Militarization and the International Arms Race in Latin America

Foreign Relations of the Third World

Militarization and the International Arms Race in Latin America

Augusto Varas

Westview Press • Boulder and London

Foreign Relations of the Third World, No. 4

Copyright © 1985 by Westview Press, Inc.

Published in 1985 in the United States of America by Westview Press, Inc., 5500 Central Avenue, Boulder, Colorado 80301; Frederick A. Praeger, Publisher

Library of Congress Cataloging in Publication Data
Varas, Augusto.
  Militarization and the international arms race in
Latin America.
  (Foreign relations of the Third World; no. 4)
  Bibliography: p.
  Includes index.
  1. Latin America—Armed Forces. 2. Latin America—
Armed Forces—Political activity. 3. Munitions—Latin
America. 4. Arms race—Latin America—History—20th
century. 5. Latin America—Military relations—Foreign
countries. I. Title. II. Series: Foreign Relations of the
Third World series; no. 4.
UA602.3.V37 1985   355'.0098   84-26987
ISBN 0-8133-0004-5

Printed and bound in the United States of America

10 9 8 7 6 5 4 3 2 1

To María Elena Valenzuela

Contents

Tables

Preface

This book expresses personal and collective apprehension over the devastating consequences of militarization and the arms race in Latin America and throughout the world.

After the military coup that overthrew the constitutional government of President Salvador Allende and the Popular Unity coalition, concern over the causes of this dramatic change in Chilean politics motivated all my intellectual endeavors. Starting in 1975, I undertook a series of research projects to explore and understand the surprising appearance of the military in local politics. Like most Chilean citizens, I have been amazed by the brutality of the coup and by the close alliance between the armed forces and groups such as the financial community. I began to work, with colleagues and friends, at the Latin American Faculty of Social Sciences (FLACSO) on the ideological, political, and institutional development of the Chilean armed forces. From these efforts emerged several published articles and books, authored by me or in collaboration with others, particularly Felipe Agüero, Fernando Bustamante, Hugo Frühling, and Carlos Portales. I wish to thank all of them for the experience of that challenging, creative process.

The general intellectual milieu at FLACSO in Santiago was extremely stimulating. I was able to benefit from a variety of collective projects, particularly the analysis of Latin American geopolitical military theory as formulated by Jorge Chateau, the analysis of the national security doctrine carried out by Manuel Antonio Garretón, and several analyses of Latin American and Chilean authoritarianism conducted by José Joaquin Brunner, Enzo Faletto, Angel Flisfisch, Norbert Lechner, and Tomás Moulian.

In order to understand the causes and antecedents of local militarization, I had to analyze the regional and international relations of the Chilean and Latin American armed forces. In this effort my work was enriched by the insights of scholars such as Genaro Arriagada in Chile; José Antonio Viera Gallo, exiled in Italy; Raimo Väyrynen in Finland; Peter Lock, Dieter Senghaas, and Ulrich Albrecht in Germany; Alain Joxe and Alain Rouquie in France; Mary Kaldor and Robin Luckham in England; Giri Dashinkar in India; Michael Klare, John Child, Alfred

Stepan, and Abraham Lowenthal in the United States; Liisa North and Peter Landstreet in Canada; Johan Galtung and Asbjørn Eide in Norway; Clovis Brigagão and Alexandre Barros in Brazil; Victor Millán; and Antonio Cavalla in Mexico. I had the opportunity to share our common concerns over global militarization through seminars, conferences, and workshops.

In addition to the intellectual support of these friends, I am grateful for the institutional and financial assistance of the Swedish Agency for Research Cooperation with Developing Countries (SAREC), the Netherlands Organization for International Cooperation and Development (NOVIB) in Holland, the Ford Foundation and the Wilson Center in Washington, D.C., the International University Exchange Fund in Switzerland, the United Nations Educational, Scientific, and Cultural Organization (UNESCO) in Paris, and the International Peace Research Association and the Center of Latin American Studies at Duke University, all of which supported some part of this long-term endeavor. Joseph Theunis and Rodrigo Egaña in Holland, David Stephen in England, and Stephen Marks in UNESCO understood the importance of my research and contributed to its progress through their support.

All of these institutional and personal relationships contributed in 1981 to the creation of the Chilean Peace Research Association (ACHIP), of which I was the first secretary general. There I benefited from stimulating discussions with Gustavo Lagos, Alberto van Klaveren, and Heraldo Muñoz, among others.

In the present volume I have incorporated and summarized several of my previously published articles and added new chapters as well. My intent is to enhance our understanding of the international economic factors and the regional political pressures fueling the tragic arms race in Latin America.

I would like to thank Nita Rous Manitzas and Frank Manitzas for their refreshing comments on the manuscript, Pamela Quick for translating the original copy, and especially Anne-Marie Smith for editing the text and suggesting important changes and corrections. Linda Powers and Enrique Hermosilla at the Wilson Center were responsible for the material production of the manuscript, Isaac Caro in Chile collected and updated the statistical information, and Rebeca Toledo typed the final manuscript.

To all these friends, colleagues, and institutions, I offer my grateful thanks.

Augusto Varas
Santiago, Chile

Militarization and the International Arms Race in Latin America

Introduction

The arms race in Latin America cannot be analyzed independently of the historical structural relationship between the armed forces and the state, the nature of civilian domination of the military. It is within this framework of civilian-military relations that we must analyze the international influences and pressures to convert the Latin American armed forces into major consumers of international war technology and products manufactured in developed countries. The increasing militarization of Latin American societies needs to be understood not only in terms of contemporary regional politics but also against the background of the historic role of the military in the original creation and early years of development of the nations of Latin America.

The Latin American states were born and consolidated within a political vacuum. Until the advent of bourgeois authoritarianism in the nineteenth century, there was no basis or foundation for the Latin American nation as such other than military power, and the republics of the region lacked an autonomous structure beyond the vague and fluid identity of armed factions and caudillos. Without an autonomous civilian profile of its own, the nation could only be identified in its earliest history with the military power that had brought it to birth. The root of bellicose patriotic ideology can be found in this substitution of armed factions for nations.

This phenomenon has been more pronounced in some countries than in others. The interregional struggles that destroyed Argentina, Mexico, Great Colombia, and even Peru were not prominent in Chile because of the weakness of its regional centers and classes. Civilian power disciplined and firmly controlled the military strongmen inherited from the anti-absolutist struggle. Yet the sense of nationality remained weak in all of the countries of Spanish America.

After independence, the defense of national sovereignty was subordinated to a domestic political role for the Latin American armed forces. Indeed, there was little need to defend the nation from outside aggressors, as potential enemies were often incapacitated by their own internal instability. Argentina bled to death in its perpetual civil war. Peru was severely weakened by its military losses to Chile and also by the

1

permanent struggle among the caudillo elite. The professional functions of the Latin American armies were gradually reduced to combating bandits and Indians or confronting each other repeatedly in political or regional disputes. The military languished in professional stagnation under the questionable tutelage of civilians.

Meanwhile, an antimilitarist ideology, shaped significantly by the writings of the intellectuals Andrés Bello, Domingo Faustino Sarmiento, Bartolomé Mitre, and many other fugitives from the disorder of civil wars, gained ground among the educated classes, contributing to an interpretation of the fundamental problems of young nations in terms of the role of the military. According to this antimilitarist political philosophy, armies are objective representatives of barbarism in the continuum between barbarism and civilization. One of the philosophy's chief aims is to minimize the role of force in political life. This position contrasts strongly with the Latin American glorification of military victories as the basis of nationality, which many civilians are uncomfortable with. The social elites had faltered through independence, finding it almost thrust upon them by a mixture of world events and by the vigorous action of the factions closely linked to the military liberators. Independence was not sought because of the ideological commitment of the social elite. It was founded instead on a culture of "war victories" that substituted for an ideological program. The antimilitarism that developed later rejected the civilian subordination to the military that the transition to independence had entailed.

The military establishment used its dominant role in the creation of the state to justify its own institutional autonomy and has resisted subordination to civilian government except in situations of clear hegemony by a strong power bloc. When civilian rule is identified with a stable order and a unified and unbroken state, the military will accept the situation, but as soon as civilian power exhibits contradictions and the state appears divided and torn apart by particular interests and parties, the military feels that its own institutional integrity may be threatened.

Latin American armed forces consequently avoided being subjected to a divided and contradictory civilian political power. The military was willing to submit itself formally only to a stable and balanced state. Any serious indecision or disagreement within the state appeared threatening and subversive to the military. During the nineteenth century the ruling class came to assert not only its political dominance, but also its control of both the state and the military, inspiring resentment from the armed forces. Military leaders from the 1930s to the 1950s used this anticivilian reaction as their principal source of legitimacy within their own headquarters. Later generations of military leaders have been astonished by the high degree of civilian control and intervention in military life that prevailed during the nineteenth century.

In some countries the military's resentment of civilian control was concealed as long as the civilian bloc in power was stable and secure and as long as the military lacked the professional values that would enable it to define its institution positively vis-à-vis the rest of society. In such cases a set of corporatist values able to repel civilian "intrusion" remained undeveloped. There was no strong basis for military autonomy, nor had the unique competence of officers to direct the military been demonstrated. In other cases, the instability of civilian domination was a more than sufficient argument to propel the military into local politics as a legitimate actor.

Despite the political instability of civilian power and the catastrophic effects of confrontations between the military and other political actors, the Latin American armed forces began a slow and occasionally inter-rupted process of professionalization at the end of the nineteenth century. This process resulted from the relative fragmentation of the economic, political, and military domination of British imperialism, and the sub-sequent emergence of sustained international competition between Eng-land, Germany, and France for control of the New World.

Rivalry between the European imperial powers and their involvement in local civil wars resulted in increasing pressure on the Latin American armed forces to accept collaboration in their process of professionalization. The French and German military missions to Latin America in this period had important political and institutional consequences. Although the Latin American armed forces continued to be seen as agencies subordinated to civilian power, increased esteem for their military virtues resulted from this professionalization and the prestige they acquired by cooperating with European armed forces.

In those countries where the process of professionalization coincided with stable civilian domination—Chile and Uruguay—the armed forces came to be seen as a national force, a faithful and true expression of society. This new army inherited the original image of the armed forces as symbiotic with the nation itself—not a mere entity superimposed upon a preexistent national organism. In the rest of Latin America military professionalization was achieved relatively free of civilian dom-ination, reinforcing the institutional autonomy of the armed forces. This was the case in Argentina, Brazil, and Peru.

Following their professionalization under the guidance of European armed forces, Latin American armies found themselves in a paradoxical and frustrating position. In countries where they submitted to firm civilian control, the armies discovered that they lacked the autonomy to pursue further development and modernization. They began to demand an accurate assessment of their professional requirements and civilian recognition of their need for autonomy. A new phase in political development began for modern Latin American armed forces once they had a corporatist base from which to launch autonomous political involvement in the state. Within this historical development, we find an increasing allocation of state financial resources for military institutions and specifically for the acquisition of ever more sophisticated and numerous armaments, fueling an accelerating arms race throughout Latin America.

The following chapters address the primary elements that allow an explanation and understanding of the phenomenon of the arms race in Latin America. The first chapter discusses the principal historical reasons for the peculiar political role of the armed forces in Latin American societies, and enumerates the reasons for their degree of institutional autonomy. The next chapter covers the development of the military ideology known as the "national security doctrine" and its contribution to the increasing autonomy of the armed forces in the latter half of the twentieth century. The third chapter addresses the factors that have been associated lately with a noticeable increase in Latin American military expenditures and the renewed impetus this has given to the regional arms race. The fourth chapter establishes the differences between domestic factors and dynamic international elements of the arms race, and this analysis continues in the fifth chapter with a study of how military technology is transferred from industrialized countries to the principal participants in the arms race of the region. Chapter 6 analyzes the military's perception of threats to national security. Taking into consideration all the elements that explain the arms race in Latin America, Chapter 7 establishes the principal steps necessary to control the growing interregional conflicts that have been unleashed as a result of increased military autonomy and the simultaneous increase in military expenditures. The eighth chapter is dedicated to analyzing the previously studied set of variables as manifested in the case of the Chilean armed forces. I chose Chile for this case study not only because of my familiarity with the country but also because it demonstrates the principal tendencies that characterize Latin American armed forces during the 1980s. The book concludes with an analysis of the factors necessary to assure the demilitarization, disarmament, and democratization of the armed forces of Latin America.

1. The Role of the Armed Forces in Latin American Societies

The political role performed by the Latin American armed forces in the twentieth century is constrained by their earlier identity and functions. The military has been historically important in the continent's struggles for independence—first from Spain's formal rule and then from its informal domination—and through this process, the military has been transformed into the guarantor of the economic liberty of national oligarchies.[1]

HISTORICAL IMAGE OF THE MILITARY

The armed forces have played an unusual role in the ideology as well as the actual formation of many Latin American states. The development of military institutions and their increasing material resources have been identified in Latin American history with the appearance and consolidation of the state—the centralized administrative political body—and the nation—the unified social body.[2]

In the nineteenth century, an image of the military as the protagonist in the formation of nations was created. The position of the nation during the formative colonial period, and later the attainment of independence and the consolidation of independent republics, were largely seen as the products of great military achievements. The official iconography of the Latin American state attributes the emergence, consolidation, and expansion of the nation to the use of arms, obscuring the context of larger global processes. This overvaluation of the military is expressed in the military establishment's image of itself as the nucleus of the nation and the skeleton of the state.

Although it ignores many other factors important to the creation of nations, this conception contains a degree of truth. In comparison with the formation of nations elsewhere in the world, the military has indeed played a disproportionately significant role in Latin America. In Europe, Japan, and the United States, the fundamental elements of national life and mythology are never military deeds or war heroes. In the French national consciousness, for example, Napoleon is not remembered as the father of the country; nor, for the German people, does the battle of Sedan merit the celebration and commemoration that Chacabuco and Ayacucho do in Latin America. The accomplishments of armies and their leaders are relatively incidental in the historical development of these European nations. The national destinies of Japan and the United States have been forged, on more than one occasion, by the use of military force, but the root of their national identity lies rather in civilian life, which through its momentum and vitality subsumes the conflicts of war. Civilian life has a richness not to be found in the military, regardless of its importance in national life. The national cohesion of the United States and the European nations rests upon the solidity and stability of civil society, the strength of a productive economy, and a clearly defined political identity shared by all social classes.

In contrast, the countries of Latin America attained independence without a legitimized class structure and lacking a rich civilian and intellectual life—almost as cardboard reconstructions of a distant Bourbon administration. They relied upon caudillos—military strongmen—to discipline the unintegrated local bourgeoisie, who lacked the political maturity to initiate autonomous national development.[3] Thus, in the history of Latin America, individual military leaders often loom larger than individual nations.

In each country that emerged from the disintegration of the Spanish Empire, weak local bourgeoisies deferred to a military chief in the hope of establishing some sort of balance between competing interests, however unstable and precarious. The Argentina of Juan Manuel de Rosas, with its protracted struggle between the centralists and federalists, is a good example, as are Bolivia under Simón Bolívar and Antonio José de Sucre, Mexico under Antonio López de Santa Anna, Ecuador under Juan José Flores, Venezuela under José Antonio Páez, and Chile under Bernardo O'Higgins.

A contradiction inevitably emerged between the interests of the local oligarchies and the projects of the grand military leaders. The latter, imbued with a universalist vision, were committed to the great historical struggle between the old regime and the revolutionary ideals of the anti-absolutist movement; whereas the local oligarchies, with their particularist views, sought only to acquire whatever benefits the colonial pact could extract from the Crown. They were unable to understand, appreciate, or support the liberating missions that the great military leaders defined. As an example of this lack of support, Argentinian statesman and hero José de San Martín, having liberated Peru, was abandoned by the Argentinian government. Bolívar, O'Higgins, José Gervasio Artigas, and Sucre suffered similar fates of neglect and exile.

The incompetence of the dominant political classes explains, in part, why military leaders were the ones to give coherence to the state in the postindependence power vacuum. The lack of politics, in the best and fullest sense of the word, left emerging nations with no recourse but to turn to the military leaders of the fight for independence, with each group seeking its own provincial chief. Struggles between regions were subsumed by struggles among military chiefs or factions, and the military faction thus became identified with the emerging nation. This phenomenon has left contemporary observers with the impression of a continent enslaved by a series of armed bands.

Military presence in Latin America crystallized as local groups began to forcibly dominate the geographically dispersed population. "Besides the formal army, in the countries that have made war beyond their borders—which is the case of Argentina, Venezuela, New Granada, and Chile—rustic militias have been formed to keep local order . . . closer to the regional power structures."[4] The military also acquired an important social role in the power struggles to fill central political positions that had been left vacant by the departing colonial governments, to consolidate national unity, and to clarify borders. The grand campaigns of Bolívar also strengthened and broadened the role of the military.

Thus the armed forces became key factors in *formal* national unity, setting limits on rivalries between diverse Latin American oligarchies or becoming the armed branch of a particular local oligarchy. The armed forces also facilitated the expansion of capitalist productive forces in dependent Latin American countries by conquering or securing territory rich in raw materials or commercial routes. Examples of such conquests are the wars of Chile with Peru and Bolivia, between Ecuador and Peru, and between the Triple Alliance of Argentina, Uruguay, and Bolivia against Paraguay.[5]

Throughout Latin America, central governments were being installed before nations were consolidated or oligarchies were solidified. There were geographic gaps between settlements and power gaps between disparate local oligarchies. The nominally governing oligarchs were in reality situated atop a heterogenous mixture of cultures and an unintegrated collection of various forms of production. These collectivities hardly merited the name of nation, nor could they be said to have national interests. The principal feature of these new political entities, besides their limited and dependent productive forces, was their lack of an identity guaranteed by the "moral and cultural leadership" of dominant oligarchies. Under such conditions, the state acquired strategic importance in the confirmation of nationality[6] and the military became fundamental in establishing state power. In Latin America, then, the state preceded the nation and the military was integral to the state.

In this process of consolidation we find the origins of the historic relationship between the propertied classes and the armed forces. The interests of small local oligarchies and later of international financial oligarchies were protected by the military. These groups came to rely on the military to balance their own political incompetence and to guarantee their access to, or domination of, the state. Via the military, local oligarchies were able to impose their own interests onto those of the state.

The armed forces were thoroughly integrated into this process. They were the only institution with interests that could be attributed to the nation, and the only body strong enough to ensure the survival of the newly created nation-states. The military thus became a crucial actor in the consolidation of national identity.

In every Latin American country the armed forces historically performed three functions: the formation of the nation, support for the expansion of dependent capitalist productive forces, and the generalization of private interests. In performing these functions, the military became the institution capable of transforming private oligarchic interests into the general interests of the nation. It became the most effective tool for weak class factions to impose their own interests on the nation. Once borders were defined and the first phase of expansion of production was complete, the process of solidifying oligarchic dominance and fabricating national interests could be pursued. In this latter process, the military came to represent the national interest and offered continuity to the governing power bloc.

The inclusion of the military in these power blocs enabled the introduction and protection of the interests of foreign capital. At the end of the nineteenth century and the beginning of the twentieth, this was part of the professionalization that the Latin American armed forces achieved under the direction of European armed forces—principally German, British, French, and Italian. Professionalization affected not only the disciplines, strategies, and weapons of the Latin American armed forces, but also their ideologies and social roles. Conceptions of the proper social role of the military were adopted from Europe with no adaptation to Latin America's very different political and economic context.[7] Some Latin American armed forces deepened their corporatist character, while others strengthened their identity with the interests of the oligarchy. The general effect was to define the military simultaneously as protector of dependent capitalism and guarantor of national unity.

The functions historically performed by the Latin American armed forces and the ideological influences that they absorbed in the process of professionalization crystallized in a particular conception of themselves. When incorporated into the instruction in war colleges, this acquired the nature and weight of a military doctrine. The armed forces viewed themselves as essential to the state, and their institution became identified and confused with the nation. This identification was the nucleus of the military institution, affecting all its later transformations and options within political struggles. Political ideologies revolved more or less around this axis.

THE CRISIS OF POLITICAL DOMINANCE

At the end of the nineteenth century and into the twentieth, Latin America suffered from prolonged economic stagnation. The exhaustion of the local dependent economy coincided with the rupture of national unity, precipitating a crisis for the nation and for the military. The failure of local productive forces seemed to the military to threaten their own functions. The gap between the military's corporate ideals (as the nucleus of the nation) and the new reality was difficult to confront. The trauma of this hiatus between the ideal and the real caused the armed forces to shift their identity from protagonists of territorial expansion to protectors of the internal political domination of these oligarchs. This allowed the military to maintain its identity with the "nation" and its close relationship with the propertied classes. With this shift in function, the military began to participate in internal politics, at first under the direction of particular caudillos, and later as a unified institution.

The transfer of the military's identity in the first decades of the twentieth century was also due to a change in local power blocs as European capital was replaced by U.S. capital and the process of industrialization was begun. The context of relatively weak and disputing elites emphasized the option of the use of force. As the armed forces became extensions of the embattled power blocs, the political struggles of the period penetrated the military institutions, fragmenting them politically and ideologically. The legitimacy of armed interventions or solutions was renewed as Latin American economies redefined their position in the international division of labor. A transformation and reconstitution of power blocs occurred in most countries between the two world wars. During this period, crises of government throughout Latin America were resolved through military coups.

Military intervention became a universal solution for any interbourgeois dispute. Through political involvement and the application of new economic and social programs, the armed forces reconditioned the old structure that had not been able to absorb or incorporate the interests of the newly created working and middle classes into the power blocs. They promoted the nationalist and populist interests of the epoch and thereby consolidated the role of the armed forces. Examples are the Juliana Revolution in Ecuador; the military intervention and first rule of Carlos Ibáñez in Chile; Getúlio Vargas's first government in Brazil; the regime of General Agustín Pedro Justo in Argentina; and the "liberal" successors to the Juan Vicente Gómez dictatorship in Venezuela, Generals López Contreras and Medina Angarita. Despite the apparently genuine intentions of these reform movements, the military presence in Latin American politics actually meant nothing more than the imposition, through the armed forces, of new propertied factions.

This involvement of the armed forces in national politics had diverse effects on the military institutions. On the one hand, the military's tendency to visualize itself as being above factional political disputes was reinforced. Because the armed forces were organically linked to the propertied factions, the fulfillment of the interests of the latter could be justified through military ideologies championing general universal interests. Also, although the armed forces cannot be considered *stricto*

sensu intellectuals, their functions as executors of the class project of
the propertied factions—the long-term strategy of economic accumulation
and political domination—placed them in that role. (Intellectuals in
Gramsci's usage are those that determine the consciousness and ideology
of the social classes.) In the context of the hegemonic crisis we have
identified, the military institutions tried not only to reconcile the differences of the emerging propertied factions, but also to impose the
interests of these factions upon the larger society.

According to Gramsci, "the division of powers and all the discussion
which has occurred about its realization and the juridical dogmatics
born from its advent are a result of the struggle between civil society
and political society of a given historical period, in a certain unstable
equilibrium of classes, established by the fact that some categories of
intellectuals (in the direct service of the state, *especially the civil and
military*) are still linked to old dominant classes."[8] However, it appears
to me that the relationship established in Latin America in the first
decades of the twentieth century linked the armed forces with the *new*
propertied factions, particularly the industrial and the intermediate
bourgeoisie. In this sense, the armed forces were "intellectuals in the
direct service of the state," which was itself a tool of the new propertied
strata.

From this point of view, the military's interventions and populism
in the period between the world wars appears to be a type of Bona-
partism;[9] however, the relationship with the emerging propertied factions
was a close, organic, and desirable tie, rather than an imposition or
necessary evil. Military interventions assisted the development of bourgeois hegemony. Emerging bourgeois factions, allied with foreign and
especially U.S. capital, dominated the military. Despite this organic
relationship, the armed forces *appeared* detached from the power bloc,
which reinforced their tendency to define themselves as an institution
capable of representing national interests. Supposedly free of any particular class link, the military was nevertheless penetrated and fragmented
by political struggles. This was evidenced by a permanent oscillation
between interventionism and formal constitutionalism.[10]

The military resolved this indecision by creating a doctrine that
included many fragments of ideology from the propertied factions that
had dominated the armed forces and also reflected the influence of the
European armed forces during the process of professionalization. The
result was a highly heterogeneous military ideology, which achieved
ideological coherence only upon incorporating specific class interests.
This fragmented and impotent doctrine was open to political manipulation
and caudillismo. If some class group or faction imposed itself momentarily
on military headquarters, the narrow interests of this faction would be
presented as "the general interest," subsuming minority interests under
national colors.

This new form of insertion into national politics impeded the armed
forces from establishing an institutional profile that could protect them

from the vicissitudes of unstable domestic politics. Military institutions continued to be relatively "available" in political terms. This contradictory position of the armed forces in Latin American societies explains the great variety of military coups on the continent through the mid-1950s.[11] Likewise, it reveals the incapacity of the political groups that temporarily influenced or managed the armed forces to promote or impose a single national program of development.

After World War II, the involvement of U.S. capital in local power blocs engendered economic and political conditions that led to three different alliances. The first alliance was established between U.S. capital and the local bourgeoisies with the purpose of consolidating the process of import substitution. A second alliance developed between the Latin American and U.S. governments. After its experience in World War II, the U.S. government felt compelled to align—although not without difficulty—with Latin American governments and thereby obtain their economic support through imports of cheap raw materials and foodstuffs. The third alliance was between the Latin American and U.S. armed forces, whose prestige following its victories around the world was indisputable.[12] (During World War II some Latin American military officers had been sympathetic to the Axis powers, and Argentina's support for the Axis powers was outright. Vargas's Brazil, in contrast, sent an expeditionary force to fight on the Allied side in Italy.)

After World War II the Latin American armed forces, under the direction of their U.S. counterparts, were integrated into the hemispheric defense system via the Interamerican Reciprocal Assistance Treaty, which was signed by the American nations in Rio de Janeiro in 1947. Although this instrument was designed to counter armed invasions from outside the hemisphere, it also contained elements that eased legitimation of U.S. intervention in the region within the framework of the Pan-American system.[13] This military alliance was perfected through the military aid pacts signed by the United States and each Latin American government in the mid-1950s. The United States channeled military aid to Latin America under the regulations of the Mutual Security Act (1953–1961) and the Foreign Assistance Act (1963).

Their alliance with the U.S. military allowed the Latin American armed forces to disengage themselves from the immediate political scene and to enter later at a higher institutional level. In the first place, it allowed the Latin American armed forces to attain greater modernization and professionalization (for data on their size, see Table 1). This was true of all Latin American countries, although the United States favored some according to its own strategic interests.[14] In the second place, U.S.-directed professionalization disseminated the ideological elements of the Cold War within the Latin American military institutions. An exaggerated anticommunism was thus inculcated into the armed forces of the continent and the potential danger of Soviet aggression was identified with the internal threat from the political left.

TABLE 1
Military Personnel in Latin American Countries, 1971-1980
(Armed Forces in Thousands and per Thousand People)

	1971		1972		1973		1974	
	1000s	per 1000	1000s	per 1000	1000s	per 1000	1000s	per 1000
Argentina	140	5.8	140	5.7	160	6.5	150	6.0
Bolivia	17	4.0	17	3.9	18	4.0	18	3.9
Brazil	375	3.8	410	4.1	420	4.1	435	4.1
Chile	70	7.4	75	7.7	75	7.6	90	9.0
Colombia	50	2.3	50	2.2	50	2.2	50	2.1
Costa Rica	2	1.1	2	1.1	2	1.1	2	1.1
Cuba	140	16.1	140	15.7	140	15.6	140	15.2
Dominican Republic	16	3.6	16	3.5	16	3.4	18	3.7
Ecuador	20	3.3	20	3.2	20	3.1	20	3.0
El Salvador	6	1.6	8	2.1	8	2.1	8	2.0
Guatemala	13	2.4	14	2.5	13	2.3	13	2.2
Honduras	8	2.9	12	4.1	12	4.0	10	3.2
Jamaica	4	2.0	4	2.0	4	2.0	4	1.9
Mexico	80	1.5	80	1.5	80	1.5	85	1.5
Nicaragua	6	3.0	6	3.0	6	2.9	6	2.9
Panama	7	4.7	7	4.4	7	4.4	8	4.7
Paraguay	15	5.8	15	5.8	15	5.6	15	5.4
Peru	75	5.4	75	5.2	75	5.1	90	6.0
Uruguay	19	6.8	20	7.1	20	7.1	25	8.9
Venezuela	45	4.1	45	3.9	50	4.2	50	4.1
Total Latin America[a]	1,125	3.9	1,173	4.0	1,208	4.0	1,248	4.1

[a]The total also includes figures for Guyana, Trinidad and Tobago, and Haiti, not listed here individually.

Source: U.S. Arms Control and Disarmament Agency, World Military Expenditures and Arms Transfers 1971-1980 (Washington, D.C.: ACDA, 1983).

Both processes—professionalization and the adoption of a new ideology—pressured the armed forces to involve themselves in society and politics. The ideological hegemony of the United States produced in the Latin American military a consensus and articulation that the propertied factions had not been able to develop, much less impose, upon the whole of society. The process of professionalization accomplished under the ideological hegemony of the United States thus *catalyzed* the heterogeneous ideological elements and allowed them to be ordered and ranked. The military established an identity and unity *apparently* independent from internal political struggles. The problems generated by

1975		1976		1977		1978		1979		1980	
1000s	per 1000	1000s	per 1000	1000s	per 1000	1000s	per 1000	1000s	per 1000	1000s	per 1000
160	6.3	155	6.0	155	5.9	155	5.8	160	5.9	160	5.8
20	4.3	22	4.6	20	4.0	20	3.9	22	4.2	24	4.5
455	4.2	450	4.1	450	4.0	450	3.9	455	3.8	455	3.7
110	10.8	111	10.7	111	10.6	111	10.4	111	10.3	115	10.5
50	2.1	60	2.4	60	2.4	60	2.3	63	2.4	65	2.6
2	1.0	3	1.5	3	1.4	3	1.4	4	1.8	4	1.7
120	12.9	125	13.2	200	20.8	210	21.6	375	38.3	375	39.1
18	3.6	19	3.7	19	3.6	19	3.5	23	4.1	23	4.0
20	2.9	24	3.4	30	4.1	35	4.7	35	4.5	35	4.4
8	2.0	8	1.9	8	1.8	10	2.3	7	1.5	8	1.7
13	2.1	14	2.2	14	2.2	14	2.1	15	2.2	15	2.1
12	3.8	12	3.6	12	3.5	13	3.9	12	3.3	12	3.2
1	0.5	1	0.5	1	0.5	1	0.7	2	1.0	2	1.0
95	1.6	100	1.7	100	1.6	145	2.3	100	1.5	110	1.6
5	2.3	5	2.2	6	2.6	n.a.	n.a.	25	10.4	50	20.0
8	4.7	8	4.4	8	4.4	8	4.4	9	4.7	11	5.8
15	5.4	15	5.2	15	5.0	15	5.0	15	4.8	15	4.7
95	6.1	100	6.3	125	7.7	125	7.5	125	7.3	150	8.5
25	8.9	28	9.7	28	9.7	28	9.7	29	10.0	29	10.0
55	4.3	55	4.2	55	4.0	55	3.9	58	4.0	58	3.4
1,297	4.1	1,328	4.1	1,436	4.3	1,500	4.4	1,662	4.8	1,734	4.9

the continuous, frustrating search for a corporatist identity came to an end. The armed forces acquired a new profile that included a higher degree of professionalism and a definite ideology. What the Latin American propertied factions had not been capable of attaining was at last achieved by U.S. instructors.

In this context, the emphasis was no longer on supporting this or that propertied faction, but on permitting and protecting the realization of the interests of the new bloc in power as a whole. Rather than supporting one oligarchic faction or party, the military came to defend capitalism as a system. This was due both to the incorporation of U.S.

capital into Latin American power blocs and to the fragmentation of the local propertied factions in each of the countries involved.

This process had several effects on the self-concept of the military. Before these changes the military had equated its interests with those of the nation, once internal divisions had been overcome. Now, the military began to define itself principally in terms of its opposition to Soviet aggression or threats. Likewise, the bourgeoisie became united by confronting antibourgeois forces. The new identity of the military and unity of the bourgeoisie were thus negative—generated by opposition to threats—rather than positive—promoting new class or institutional projects.

By the 1960s, coups and dictatorships by individuals declined and Latin America began to experience dictatorships by the entire military institution.[15] Military governments replaced traditional caudillismo. The coups in Peru (1962 and 1968), Ecuador (1963), and Brazil (1964) are examples of this new kind of regime. Governments were led by members of the army's high command, and the state apparatus was organized around them. They sought to introduce serious reforms and establish social and economic order. Whatever their specific orientation, these new military regimes were the result of a unique configuration of national and international alliances. They participated in the capitalist system of the international division of labor and allowed the investment of foreign transnational capital. They were often closely linked with U.S. foreign and military policies. The process of professionalization led to greater institutional autonomy of the military and coincided with crises in the civilian direction of state. This process was definitively articulated in the "national security doctrine" discussed in the next chapter.

NOTES

1. As Halperin put it, "the new republics arrive at independence with too many or abundant officers' corps and they almost never get rid of them." Tulio Halperin, *Historia contemporánea de América Latina* (Madrid: Alianza Editorial, 1967).

2. Some of the material presented here recapitulates the introductory chapter of Augusto Varas, Felipe Agüero, and Fernando Bustamante, *Chile, democracia, fuerzas armadas* (Santiago, Chile: FLACSO, 1980).

3. For an analysis of the permanent tension between administrative-political centralization and the tendency toward corporatism, see Claudio Veliz, *The Centralist Tradition in Latin America* (Princeton, N.J.: Princeton University Press, 1980), and Howard Wiarda, *Corporatism and National Development in Latin America* (Boulder, Colo.: Westview Press, 1982).

4. Halperin, *Historia contemporánea*, p. 37.

5. On the general political functions of the armed forces in the creation of the Third World nation-states, see Anouar Abdel-Malek, *La dialéctica social* (Mexico City: Siglo XXI, 1975).

6. For a more general analysis on the subject, see Norbert Lechner, *Estado y política en América Latina* (Mexico City: Siglo XXI, 1981).

7. Especially important in this respect were Baron Colmar von der Goltz, "El pueblo en armas" (Paris, 1883), and Luis Hubert Gonzalve Lyautey, "Du rôle social de l'officier," *Revue des Deux Mondes*, March 15, 1881, according to Frederic Nunn, "El profesionalismo militar chileno en el siglo XX," *Cuadernos del Instituto de Ciencias Políticas* (Universidad Católica de Chile), no. 9 (March-April 1976).

8. See Halperin, *Historia contemporánea*, and Guillermo Boils, "Tendencias reformistas de los militares latinoamericanos en el período entre guerras" (National University of Mexico, Mexico City, 1977), manuscript. Emphasis added.

9. See Antonio Gramsci, *Oeuvres choisies* (Paris: Éditions Sociales, 1959), p. 282.

10. For an analysis of this category applied to political analysis, see Alain Rouquie, "L'Hypotèse 'Bonapartiste' et l'emergence des systemes politiques semi-competitifs," *Revue Française des Sciences Politiques* 25, no. 6 (December 1975). See also his *Les états militaires en Amérique Latine* (Paris: Éditions du Seuil, 1982).

11. *Formal constitutionalism* refers to the political conception of liberal democratic institutions as free of class interests and therefore inherently capable of implementing national and majority interests.

12. See William Stokes, "Violence as a Power Factor in Latin American Politics," in Robert Tomasek, comp., *Latin American Politics* (New York: Doubleday, 1966). On the political meaning of the military interventions of the 1950s and 1960s, see Rodrigo Baño, "El conflicto político en América Latina," *Documento de Trabajo*, FLACSO, Santiago, 1977.

13. Edwin Lieuwin, "The Changing Role of the Armed Forces: An Analysis," in Tomasek, *Latin American Politics*.

14. Such was the case in 1964 when Cuba was expelled from the Organization of American States (OAS) and subjected to a trade embargo. The adoption of these measures has awakened serious doubts: See Claudio Grossman, "The U.N. and the OAS: Some Competence Issues in the Peace and Security Field," Ph.D. diss., Utrecht University, 1982.

15. For a deeper analysis of the Latin American military see Abraham Lowenthal, ed., *Armies and Politics in Latin America* (New York: Holmes and Meier, 1976), especially the chapters by José Nun, "The Middle-Class Military Coup Revisited"; Robert Putnam, "Toward Explaining Military Intervention in Latin American Politics"; Philippe Schmitter, "Military Intervention, Political Competitiveness, and Public Policy in Latin America: 1950–1967"; Liisa North, "The Military in Chilean Politics"; Alfred Stepan, "The New Professionalism of Internal Warfare and Military Role Expansion." See also Guillermo O'Donnell, "Las fuerzas armadas y el estado autoritario de Cono Sur de América Latina," in Lechner, *Estado y política*; Alfred Stepan, *The Military in Politics: Changing Patterns in Brazil* (Princeton, N.J.: Princeton University Press, 1971); David Collier, "Overview of the Bureaucratic-Authoritarian Model," in David Collier, ed., *The New Authoritarianism in Latin America* (Princeton, N.J.: Princeton University Press, 1979).

Two different views on the relationship between politics and the military, from a Latin American perspective, are Antonio Cavalla, *Estados Unidos–América Latina: Fuerzas armadas y defensa nacional* (Mexico: Universidad Autónoma de Sinaloa, 1980); and Genaro Arriagada, *El pensamiento político de los militares* (Santiago: CISEC, 1981). For more references on the same matter see the bibliography.

2. A Corporatist Ideology for the Latin American Military: The National Security Doctrine

In this chapter I will analyze the ideological components and effects of the "national security doctrine" in Latin America. By referring to this doctrine in the singular, I do not mean to imply that there is but one uniquely articulated doctrine, identical across national boundaries. Historical particularities of each nation have been incorporated into the ideology, but despite the resulting permutations, there are some essential elements common to all military ideologies in Latin America that espouse "national security" as their ultimate justification and goal. These elements are central to the following discussion of the doctrine of national security.[1]

GEOPOLITICS AND THE STATE

Those concepts of the military doctrine of national security that derive from geopolitics are concerned with the expansion and reordering of states and societies. Geopolitics may be said to address the dynamic relationship between the society/polity and the territory/geography of a nation, always with reference to its larger global context. Geopolitics uses a particular, elaborate, and multifaceted definition of the state. The essential elements of the state include its people (their number and strength as well as their cultural and ethnic identity), its territory (size and natural wealth as well as location in relation to the rest of the world), and its sovereignty (independence and freedom to pursue its own political destiny, both domestic and international).

The state in this conception is essentially a biogeographic phenomenon identified with the human beings that inhabit it. It is "a biological organism with a life and consciousness of its own, that is born, grows, and dies in the context of struggles and biological conflicts."[2] In an elaboration of this organic conception of the state as a superbeing, the heartland is the nucleus; the hinterland is the surrounding tissue that nourishes the nucleus; the borders or periphery form the epidermis; and the communication network is the nervous system. As a superbeing, the state has a typical life cycle of birth, growth, and death. The most important stage is that of growth—in geopolitical terms, development and expansion. These are not superlative achievements but rather the natural activities of the state, just as survival is its principal instinct.

This paradigm of the life cycle encapsulates the geopolitical conception of the state. Its overall objective is to maximize "the well-being of the people." Toward this end, geopolitics defines the "science" and "laws" whereby the best policies to achieve these ends may be identified. This science presupposes a leadership and political discourse capable of articulating or realizing the will of the state and implementing the scientifically determined policies. In this way, survival is ensured and growth and "well-being" optimized.

Other factors integral to this geopolitical world view are national security, military power, development, and sovereignty. Sovereignty is the capacity of the state to transform itself, while growing, without losing its identity. Any state with a healthy survival instinct cannot accept subjugation to another, as this would be a loss of sovereignty and identity. Sovereignty is, then, a concept abstracted from particular geopolitical situations; it is a faculty indispensable to a state's self-identity within all the phases of the life cycle.

The concepts of "sovereign power" or "national power" are based on this understanding.

> The force which organizes social life, in the broadest sense of the state, is constituted by "national power." This is an organic force with which the state pursues and directs its destiny. "Power," then, is the capacity of the population to exploit and administer the space it inhabits and to articulate and fulfill, in an essentially dynamic way, the will of the state.[3]

Power includes not merely physical force, but also the material capacities of the population and its collective spiritual, intellectual, and creative strength. Taken together, these form what is called the national power of a state.

NATIONAL SECURITY AND THE INTERNAL FRONT

The concept of national power informs the organizational aspect of the national security doctrine, as applied to both the "internal front" (society) and the military. It is oriented toward realizing sovereignty and freeing the state to pursue its life cycle. Within the doctrine of national security, the concept of internal front either refers simply to the population, or, in addition, to "the social groups and basic institutions of the state."[4] The internal front includes people who are not prepared to handle arms in defense of the state, but who provide the armed forces with strategic and moral support. Other elements of the internal front include territory, natural resources, sociological identity (literacy, density of population, political homogeneity), nature of government, industrial capacity, and national morale.[5]

Within the doctrine of national security, all of these elements are considered to be within the sphere of the military—an impressive range. The process by which the armed forces and the political leadership perceive or define the needs and preferences of a society is understood as simple, direct, and unimpeded by circumstance. "National objectives" are seen as "the goals and needs (as selected and analyzed by the government) that a people wish to reach in a determined period of time, whether by peaceful or by forcible means."[6] The involvement of the armed forces is incorporated into the very definition of the goals of the people and the state, and the intervention of the armed forces is imperative when these objectives (as evaluated by the military) are threatened.

National security is thus broadly construed as "the objectives of a sovereign country and the coordination of civilian activities with the armed forces, with the end of preserving national independence and integrity."[7] These key concepts may be weighed and defined differently in each country, military, or branch of the armed forces, accounting for the differences among the policies that are "deduced" from this ideology throughout Latin America.

The concept of the internal front may be extended to include "integral security." This concerns the deterioration of civilian moral, intellectual, and physical capacities, if they become so inferior as to threaten the existence and development of the state. These geopolitical elements affect the "health" of the state, and the pursuit of integral security entails "procedures to monitor it and opportunely detect 'illnesses' and their suitable treatment so as to guarantee a long, secure, and normal evolution."[8] "Integral security" is thus more comprehensive than "national security." It includes the safety of the state from either external or internal threats against its territorial integrity, authority, and institutions. Such threats may be present or future, and this doctrine tends to downplay the positive contributions of civilians toward achieving national objectives, dwelling instead on the civilian tendency toward moral and intellectual decadence and the risk at which this may put the institutions of the state.

Positive development of civilian capability is nonetheless a necessary precursor to the growth of the state. All civilian capabilities, however, must be infused with a commitment to "homeland and patriotism." This becomes an organic necessity; it is "the common sentiment that orients the interests of the citizens toward one sole national objective. . . . a powerful moral force, a true motor and lever of the progress of a state."[9] This sentiment is promoted through reverence for the emblem and symbols of the nation, its traditions and heroes, as well as an adequate civil-military education.

National security thus addresses the most diverse aspects of the life of a society in order to organize and control them. In geopolitical terms, the concepts of national security and integral security inform the principal duties of the state. A national security doctrine, then, is the set of government policies that seeks to elevate and strengthen the best aspects (from the point of view of a particular actor) of the people/territory (or blood/earth) dyad within a nation. The goal is a solid national power capable of guaranteeing the sovereignty of the state as it grows and develops.

In applying this concept of national security to the problems of economic development, geopolitics fundamentally relates economic and social development to security. These are equally important and reciprocally supportive. Development and security are thus two sides or aspects of the same project and may be said to "constitute equally important motives for the evolution and growth of states."[10] They must be adequately balanced and closely related in a program that enhances civilian cultural capacities while building national defensive and productive powers.

The relationship that is established between national security and development derives from the geopolitical commitment to autarchy, or self-rule. To ensure sovereignty, a state must be self-sufficient in raw materials and foodstuffs, as well as in the industrial inputs necessary for the development of national power. Political insurgency or opposition threatens both security and development, and is seen as a product of civilian failure to overcome acute social inequalities. Third World governments must thus provide solutions to both underdevelopment and insurgence.

Although there are many variations within geopolitical ideology, most ideologies construe development as the best weapon against subversion in underdeveloped countries, affirming a causal relationship between underdevelopment and the tendency of a state to use violence: "The poor and underdeveloped countries of the southern hemisphere are a permanent source of conflict, and their pacification can only be achieved with a new security concept which is development."[11]

Diverse factors have been grafted onto the original conception of national security. The ideological character of new forms of conflict, internal subversion, and psychological warfare have led to the idea of "total war," requiring the commitment and involvement of all citizens in this new type of warfare. National security thus entails the ability of a nation to marshal adequate internal, external, psycho-social, and military resources to produce a solid national power capable of guaranteeing state sovereignty in the fulfillment of its objectives of development and security. The nation must defend itself against any conduct defined as subversion that would lead to the disintegration of the state— as understood by this ideology.

THE IDEOLOGY OF NATIONAL SECURITY

This synthesis of the principal elements of the military's national security doctrine permits us to appreciate its implicit ideological premises. Although we will not attempt to dismantle all the ideological machinery, we will elucidate the historical development of this doctrine and characterize its principal consequences at both political and social levels in Latin American countries.

In the historical development of the doctrine, certain elements that were incorporated into military ideology immediately after World War II reflected the experiences of the armed forces during the war. There was a new sense of the "enemy" that went beyond the formal army of an opposing sovereign state to include guerrilla forces or the people of an occupied country. The significant involvement of civilian populations in World War II (the French resistance under the Vichy regime, the partisan resistance in Yugoslavia and Poland) changed the character of modern war, giving it a new profile—in military terms called total warfare. As the civilian population became involved in military actions, new weapons and tactics were developed to confront this new enemy. The concept of total war emerged from this experience, from the need to combat civilian participation in the war at all levels and to develop a variety of tactics, including psychological warfare.

Through the bipolar configuration of powers that followed World War II, capitalism and socialism became thoroughly identified with the United States and the Soviet Union respectively. All geopolitical or military disputes were immediately forced into this bipolar grid. Contradictions within imperialism and competition between imperialist powers—the cause of wars during the nineteenth and twentieth centuries—were subordinated to the confrontation between the two different models of organizing production and society. The nature of confrontation changed from open armed conflict to ideological antagonism, commercial competition, military posturing, and the arms race. In the context of the Cold War, the enemy could be characterized more by its ideology than by its nationality. Given the bipolar understanding of ideology, only two categories were available. The inherent conflict between capital and labor was worked out in each society not only in the context of its own history, politics, and material resources, but also in this global context of the dichotomy of ideologies.

In Latin America, fear of communism was transferred from fear of Soviet invasion to fear of internal subversion. Leftist forces identified in any way with socialist ideologies were simply eliminated from political pacts. Local communist parties were persecuted and outlawed. The military concept of total warfare fit smoothly into this ideological dichotomy as applied to the nation. The notion of internal war was thus introduced and consolidated.

Within the overarching ideological framework of the Cold War, a number of subcomponents were identified: the four fronts (war, internal, international, and economic), the coordination of fronts in case of a war emergency, and the necessity of including the military in all decisions that might in some way affect national defense. However, because national defense involves not only the military but also the total population and national and international resources, and because the war effort necessitates preparation, a corollary was developed that stated that countries must always be ready for military confrontation and that this readiness must include and impinge upon all national activities. The war effort was thus converted into the principal organizing factor of society.

The ideology developed to elaborate and justify this political strategic orientation was the ideology of national security. As it developed, this doctrine focused on the military as the instigator and guide of social action at every level. Before World War II, the armed forces had been under civilian power and lacked their own unique set of doctrines. Within these limits, they could elaborate but not change or guide their functions or their role of maintaining national sovereignty and defense. During the professionalization and modernization of the military subsequent to World War II, a corporatist ideology emerged from military headquarters that transformed the military way of seeing the world and of situating themselves in it. The theory of society developed by the armed forces was nothing more than the limited freedom or rationale that they would grant to civil society and its practices.

This military theory reflects the great distance between the intellectual cadres of the military and civilian power. Outdated organicism and its consensual view of society, handed down through German instruction, was combined with notions of national interest introduced by U.S. training. Latin American military doctrines did not emerge from a consideration and analysis of Latin American societies, but instead received their first impulse from foreign military doctrines.

In the military's national security doctrine, the duty of the soldier is defined as the internal and external defense of the state. Global society is seen as an organism in which all the parts play a complementary role. In this organic view, any divergent activity is considered intrinsically harmful, as it compromises the presumed a priori equilibrium. The armed forces play a fundamental role in protecting the social system from its enemies and becomes, consequently, the central apparatus of the state, for the survival of the whole social system depends upon its adequate functioning. The military is the spinal column of society. It determines the very survival of society in a world of aggression governed by the law of survival of the fittest. Its institution and functions are glorified in the terms of science, technology, and professionalism.[12]

Within this world view, the soldier is an active agent of development and security, equipped with sophisticated tools to protect, propel, and direct the state. In this transcendent image, the soldier must eliminate from his terminology any reference to particular class interests or social forces. This emptying of classist interest from the military discourse is achieved through identifying the military with the state and identifying the values of national defense with those of the whole society. National security is universalized, and its active subjects are the members of the armed forces, whose social function is likewise universalized. Individual actions and events acquire rationality only within the universal rationality of national security, with which they must be coordinated—by the military, the bearer of national interest.

From this perspective the soldier no longer has a specialized military mission. The military becomes the essence or core of the social organism, and the military doctrine of national security manages to link all social practices to the problems of internal and external defense and to infuse the entire society with this perspective. At a less formal level, this invasion of civilian existence by military existence demands a new model of civil-military relations.

This military ideology has developed slowly but persistently throughout the twentieth century. When the armed forces, for internal political reasons, assume state control, actual policies are derived from this doctrine. A national security system is elaborated as these policies are formulated and implemented.

Although key elements of the national security ideology originated in German and U.S. contexts and were delivered as doctrine within the curricula of war colleges, they were fully formulated and effectuated by Latin American armed forces in their own societies and political activities. Because the doctrine was interpreted distinctly by each branch of the armed forces, doctrinal heterogeneity prevailed among the armed forces whether or not they were in charge of the state. Although the fundamental elements of the doctrine reached all of the forces, the internal tendency was to emphasize and project particular elements. Special cadres of officers within the war colleges were formed to homogenize, unify, and develop the doctrines. Within the framework of common ideological components, these processes of differentiation and homogenization continue.

The development of the national security doctrine entailed a new model of civil-military relations called security power. When the military is in power, it attempts not only to unite the armed forces, but also to inculcate all of society with military doctrines. This requires the explicit formulation and communication of all doctrines. In this process of educating and disciplining the whole of society, the national security doctrine has become elaborate and consistent.

We thus see an important distinction between doctrines as they exist at a military level and as they are elaborated once the military assumes control of the government. At the first level, the doctrine may provide a new model of civil-military relations. At the second, through implementation and political projection, the doctrine is no longer characteristically military, but becomes a theoretical basis for a new, nonrepublican political ideology. Under a military government, there is an effort to instill the theories and values of national security in every citizen. In the end, the governing armed forces provide ideological coherence and a nonliberal, nonrepublican homogeneity to a multiplicity of real class factions. In this way, ideological union is achieved between the armed forces, which are institutionally oriented toward politics, and those sectors of society that perceive the armed forces as oriented toward supraindividual, universalist ends that are free of specific class interests. This ideological alliance has been realized in recent years in right-wing military governments that are sustained jointly by the armed forces and by their ideological allies in civilian society.

In Latin America, early European geopolitical influences (especially German) were combined with the geopolitics implicit in U.S. Cold War formulations and the concepts derived from the professionalization implemented by U.S. armed forces. In a Latin American context of political crisis and weak civilian government, this produced a military ideology that launched the armed forces into the quest for political power, and justified their involvement. This ideological factor plays a central role in the current arms race. The crisis of the state and the excessive autonomy of the military that is associated with it are of the next chapter.

NOTES

1. This chapter is based on the critical study of national security doctrines developed originally in Augusto Varas and Felipe Agüero, *El proyecto político militar* (Santiago: FLACSO, 1984). It makes use of the principal geopolitical concepts developed by Jurgel, *Segurança e democracia;* Ejército del Ecuador, "El ejército en el desarrollo nacional"; Gallegos, "Triunfo en Perú"; Guglialmelli, "Las fuerzas armadas en América Latina"; Mercado-Jarrín, "La política de seguridad integral"; Rodriguez, "Seguridad nacional en el Ecuador"; Villegas, *Políticas y estrategias para el desarrollo y la seguridad nacional;* Pinochet, *Geopolítica;* and von Chrismar, *Leyes que se deducen del estudio de la expansión de los estados.*

See also Chateau, "Características principales del pensamiento geopolítico chileno"; Comblin, *The Church and the National Security States;* de Andrade, "Nuevas formas de hegemonía militar en América Latina" and "Sobre la actual ideología de la seguridad nacional"; Garretón, "De la seguidad nacional a la nueva institucionalidad"; Nina, "La doctrina de seguridad nacional"; Rojas and Viera-Gallo, "La doctrina de la seguridad nacional y la militarización de la política en América Latina"; Ruz, "Doctrina de seguridad nacional en América Latina"; and Varas, "Estudio comparativo de las doctrinas de seguridad nacional en algunos países de América Latina" (see bibliography for full publication data).

2. Julio von Chrismar, *Leyes que se deducen del estudio de la expansión de los estados* (Santiago: Memorial del Ejército de Chile, 1975), p. 34.

3. Augusto Pinochet, *Geopolítica* (Santiago: Editorial Andrés Bello, 1974), p. 153.

4. Rafael Zavalla Carbo, "El frente interno en la estrategia general," *Memorial del Ejército* (March-April 1969).

5. Authors in the field of geopolitics (see note 1 above) have broken the concept of national power down in different ways, but all have been guided by the "political realism" of Hans Morgenthau, *La lucha por el poder y la paz* (Buenos Aires: Ed. Sudamericana, 1963). The first U.S. edition of this book has become a study text for the Latin American armed forces.

6. René Cabrera, "Gestación del objetivo político," *Memorial del Ejército* (November-December 1955).

7. Ibid.

8. Von Chrismar, *Leyes que se deducen del estudio de la expansión de los estados,* p. 35.

9. Alberto Polloni, *Las fuerzas armadas de Chile en la vida nacional* (Santiago: Editorial Andrés Bello, 1972), p. 44.

10. Osiris Villegas, *Políticas y estrategias para el desarrollo y la seguridad nacional* (Buenos Aires: Editorial Pleamar, 1969), p. 109.

11. Peter Althaus, "La evolución de la doctrina militar norteamericana después de 1945," *Memorial del Ejército de Chile,* no. 356 (July-August 1970).

12. This conceptualization of national security doctrines was developed originally in Augusto Varas and Fernando Bustamante, *Fuerzas armadas y política en Ecuador* (Quito, Ecuador: Editora Latinoamericana, 1978).

3. The Militarization of Latin America

The arms race in the Latin American region received an important impetus from the emergence of several right-wing military governments during the 1960s and 1970s. The notoriety that the arms race has acquired on the continent is associated with the tendency of the armed forces to confront international problems by turning immediately to armed confrontation and military might to resolve all tensions and disputes. Contempt for negotiation and multilateral institutions and a neglect of international norms and bilateral agreements characterize the ruling armed forces in Latin America.

Despite the close relationship that exists between the type of political regime and the arms race, previous studies of the arms race in the region have been primarily descriptive. They have not sufficiently considered the arms buildup from a theoretical perspective, or identified its political, economic, and social factors. The shortcoming of mere description—although fundamental in initiating an approach to the arms race—is that it leads to no profound comprehension of this complex dynamic. For that one must trace the significant sources of the arms race in Latin America in both regional and global contexts, achieving in the process a fuller appreciation of not only the arms race but also Latin American society as a whole.

For this reason, I begin my analysis *within* national frameworks. From this perspective, the regional and international context is seen as contributing to but not explicitly causing the arms race. Regional and international elements are necessary but not sufficient factors in the Latin American arms race. To understand *why* the arms spiral was generated, one must focus on the environment from which it originates and identify those social sectors that assume both the cost of, and more importantly, the social responsibility for, the arms race.

The optimism of the economic and social projections for Latin America in the 1960s proved excessive. The continent has proceeded in, if not totally opposite, at least distinctly variant directions from the predicted course. The tendency toward democracy, symmetrical and concomitant with stable development, has been weakened by increasing international indebtedness.[1] And as a result of either swift and unequivocal military coups or a slower process of gaining key state positions, the armed forces have acquired important posts in national governments throughout Latin America, and are now directing or influencing state economic and political policies.

Examples abound. For the first time in several decades, the Mexican armed forces are viewed by some civilian sectors as a valid political actor. In Venezuela, despite strict subordination to civilian power, the armed forces are acquiring some control of industries, including the strategically important state oil industry. The Ecuadorian armed forces, having achieved a political-constitutional statute in the new democratic order that governs that country, have become highly independent bodies, difficult to keep under civilian control. Although their Bolivian, Colombian, Panamanian, and Peruvian peers have not acquired the same level, the political importance that the armed forces of these countries have retained even after returning power to civilians is undeniable. Elsewhere, the action of the armed forces in national politics is direct and un-mediated—in Brazil, Chile, Uruguay, and Paraguay.

Despite the diverse circumstances surrounding the new emergence of the armed forces in regional politics, there has been one common element: the explicit restriction of the scope of internal politics. Whether owing to leftist populism and anti-Americanism or rightist support of entrepreneurial projects, the institutional interference of the military in politics has limited civilian participation—through which compromise and agreements among social groups had been achieved—by restrictions on both the range of permissible action and on access to political involvement among the general population. The performance of political tasks historically reserved for civil society has been assumed by the armed forces, restricted, or eliminated altogether.

This democratic involution reflects the explicit militarization of Latin American societies. Other manifestations of this process are systematic repression of civilians by the armed forces and typically military developments such as the arms race. The concrete elements of the arms race are regular increases in military budgets, greater imports of modern weapons, larger numbers of troops, and the consolidation and development of a diversified local military industry. An analysis of these tendencies leaves no room to doubt their pertinence.[2]

The militarization of Latin American societies entails both growing military power—a response to multiple political-diplomatic and economic situations both regional and extracontinental[3]—and growing military involvement in, and control of, domestic politics. This is one of the most notable aspects of Latin American militarism: its simultaneous determination by international martial contexts and local political exigencies. The armed forces are requesting and receiving an increasingly greater share of fiscal resources as their capacity to influence governmental decision-making grows. Greater political clout translates into higher levels of state financial resources, which validates their involvement in governmental management.

Militarization, then, may be achieved directly by a military government or indirectly, through the growing capacity of the armed forces to elevate their interests, values, and duties to the level of national activities. Thus, the collective and general national interest of societal classes and groups is converted into an authoritatively defined national interest, in which the concepts of sovereignty are reinterpreted and elaborated geopolitically.[4] And just as the military increasingly manipulates the civilian government, civilian interest groups and their representatives in governments have begun to use military reasoning and military pressure in their domestic and foreign policies.

THE ARMS RACE AND THE ARMED FORCES

The arms race, which has tremendous social relevance for Latin America and all regions of the Third World, is but one expression of the larger problem of militarization. Crises over political dominance of the state in Latin American societies have played a central role in the unfolding of this process during the past decade. Militarization can be defined as an overemphasis on the importance of armed forces, and one of its manifestations is the ongoing buildup of arms. Interestingly, the same factors that relate the crisis of social direction to militarism also have pertinent effects on the arms spiral. Three significant factors stand out: the contrast between the historical role of the armed forces in Latin American nations and their current role; their self-assigned ideological function in these contexts; and their excessive autonomy within the state in times of crisis.

Along with their participation in international wars and activities of internal repression, the armed forces of Latin America have also been integrated into broad projects of social domination. Although such projects have historically been characterized by instability, the current secular crisis of hegemony has resulted in the utter predominance of the military element in Latin American societies. This situation contrasts with that in other equally fragmented societies, where the military has kept out of politics.[5] (Examples are Austria, Belgium, the Netherlands, Switzerland, and Yugoslavia.)

Initially, the rise in military expenditures was due not to the secular political crisis but to periodic increases in response to regional circumstances and to the cost of technological innovations in war materials. What is different about the current situation in Latin America is that increases in defense budgets are now being sustained relatively independent of the situation of local, regional, and international politics.

The arms race is associated with the growing strength of entrepreneurial elements within the ruling elites, and with their considerable financial resources and political ambitions. The new dynamic that this introduced into existing power blocs was not lost on the armed forces, as we shall see. Before focusing fully on this aspect of the problem, however, it is necessary to examine more closely the relationship of these new entrepreneurs to national political and economic processes.

In periods of oligarchic domination the question of sovereignty tends to be confused or fused with the question of hegemony. The oligarchy equates the maintenance of a free and sovereign territory to the continuation of its own dominance. A parallel tendency emerged among the industrial sectors, for whom maintenance of economic zones, tariffs, and customs barriers became essential to their own survival and success. The territory of capitalist accumulation coincided with national borders or frontiers.

During the 1970s a series of changes at the world level generated a new predominance of financial sectors over productive activities. Entrepreneurs acquired unprecedented influence upon ruling elites. This hypertrophy of the financial sectors is one aspect of the crisis of the international monetary system, of which the political counterpart is the fragmentation of world political power[6] and the resulting difficulties in creating a new international economic order.

The measures adopted by the Nixon administration in August 1971, including floating the dollar, initiated a series of changes of key importance to Latin American countries.[7] Since that time, industrialized countries have been unable to reestablish the international monetary system founded in Bretton Woods in 1944. Neither the realignment of currencies, nor the joint floating system, nor the definition of basket values for special drawing rights have been able to account for the new economic realities and changing power relations among principal industrial powers of market economies. As a consequence, protectionism has damaged and impeded relations both among developed countries and between developed nations and the nations of the South. A variety of restrictions such as tariffs, quotas, customs valuations, and technical controls have been instituted.

Meanwhile, rampant inflation deepens the world recession. According to René Villareal, this inflation may be traced to the

> unusual increment in military expenditures, the excessive liquidity coming from the overpowering role of the dollar as the medium of payment and international reserve, the expansion of a private type of credit through the recycling of petrodollars in the market of the Eurodollar, and the increase in the price of gold as a source of growth in the value of world reserves.[8]

Petroleum exporters have not been able to recirculate their surpluses effectively owing to the limitations of their industrial bases, increasing international liquidity. It is in this context of overliquidity that the international financial market is modified and integrated, so that an ever smaller group of financial actors tends to maximize its profits jointly at an international level.[9] Overliquidity enabled developing countries, non-exporters of petroleum, to obtain foreign financing—but only from private sources, with higher interest rates and shorter terms.[10]

In Latin America, the implications of this new situation have varied according to the type of economy of each country. For economies that depend on the export of raw materials and some manufactured products, inflation, world recession, and the new protectionism have led to a drop in exports, trade deficits, and foreign indebtedness.[11] In petroleum exporting countries, both limitations on their industrialization and the free-trade policies of Latin America inhibited their industrial options and produced harsh trade and payment deficits, also resulting in high levels of indebtedness. This was the case in Ecuador, Bolivia, Mexico, and Venezuela.[12] Villareal has observed that

> the long-term debt in favor of private creditors increased at a more accelerated rhythm than the debt to official creditors and it is estimated that it represented around 50% of total indebtedness (for non-petroleum exporting countries) at the end of 1979. . . . Of this private type of debt four-fifths correspond to financial institutions, predominantly international private banking institutions.[13]

The relevance of this new global monetary situation to the central issue of Latin American militarization is that it accentuates the political clout of those linked with international finance and capable of channeling its surpluses. The specific political weight of these actors has increased notably, whether they are maintaining capital flow under new conditions or renegotiating past unpaid balances. Most importantly, these national financial sectors now determine how a particular nation will adjust to changing global economic and political realities.

In Chile the alteration was drastic, involving a military coup; in the Brazilian postcoup period, the growing power of the financial sector led to increasing control of local economies by transnational corporations. In Argentina, inflation, abundant credit, and a deep reform of the money market generated a zenith of speculation that had potent internal political effects.[14] In Mexico the global crisis of the financial system reverberated in the tremendous devaluation of the peso, the ultimate nationalization of the banking industry, and the implementation of a recessive economic policy that reverses the historic function of the Mexican state in regulating the nation's economy. The Venezuelan response to the global situation included monetarist policies and a sizable devaluation of currency, which strongly affected the outcome of the presidential elections in 1983. The common denominator among all the examples is the influence of the private banking industry upon those in power and its growing prominence in the local economy.[15]

This shift in power within national power blocs has encouraged the armed forces to increase their participation in domestic politics. They have established a new system of political relations and are redefining their functions within the newly emerging power centers.

For the financial entrepreneurs, the importance of sovereign economic borders is downplayed, in contrast to the priorities of agriculturalists and industrialists. The financial entrepreneur prefers complete mobility of production factors, in order to take advantage of the best factors, prices, and markets, wherever they may be located. This disregard for national borders is coupled with a high valuation of the state as an instrument to facilitate the process of accumulation.

What is sensible and coherent for the financial sectors—a market without borders and a strong state—seems paradoxical to the armed forces and is difficult for them to digest. From an ideological viewpoint then, relations between these newly powerful groups and the armed forces is somewhat discordant, although cordial. The lack of ideological coherence has led the armed forces to develop their own analyses and to implement their own programs. The old national security doctrine that defined proper military action in national-civic questions has been altered by new concepts and strategies generated by the armed forces themselves.

Because the newly powerful financial sectors lack hegemonic designs on territory per se, inasmuch as this does not affect their frontiers of accumulation, they tend to devalue territorial disputes. Other concepts of great importance to the armed forces and typical of national security doctrines, such as self-government or self-sufficiency, are also questioned by financial sectors. Instead, the ideology of the financial sector emphasizes monetary assets and international currency over the ownership of natural or industrial resources. Financial technocrats argue the benefits of abundant monetary resources, allocated to military expenditures and to investment in domestic industry. They tend to promote reductions in all expenditures except military investment and to demand balanced budgets (unless confronting inflation that would upset their own stability) that limit the scope of state investment.[16] Public expenditures, diminished in real terms, are then redistributed internally. In the process, the military usually manages to enlarge its portion of the whole pie, increasing its budget in real terms. This situation is observed in Argentina, where military expenditures reached 17 percent of total expenditures in 1979; in Brazil, 20.4 percent in 1975; in Chile, 31 percent in 1979; and in Peru, 33.1 percent in 1977.[17]

Because of the obvious benefits of alliance with the entrepreneurial sectors, the armed forces favor that group within the power bloc. They are willing to overlook the financial sector's ideological disregard for territorial integrity in exchange for a larger slice of the budget. As the military grows in physical strength and prestige, it can reintroduce the issue of territorial integrity as an object of popular nationalism. This is one of the major sources of nationalism in an increasingly transnational context.

In the face of these contradictions, the armed forces realize that borders previously won by force may yet be imperiled. This volatile issue could lead to further armed confrontation. As the civilian government ignores this danger, the armed forces assume the exclusive role of territorial defense. To prepare for this eventuality, the military has sought to amass huge amounts of highly sophisticated weaponry.

This situation can be observed in Argentina, Chile, Ecuador, Uruguay, and Venezuela. In the case of Brazil, its transnational development strategy calls for broadening the boundaries of capitalist accumulation. By locating industries in border regions, Brazil has begun to integrate territories, establishing active borders that do not always coincide with its historical boundaries with Paraguay and Bolivia. Brazil, Argentina, Chile, Peru, and Venezuela accounted for almost 80 percent of Latin American military expenditures in 1982. In sum, the devaluation of territorial issues by the newly dominant financial factions has not caused the armed forces to limit their weapons or disarm. On the contrary, they have pitched themselves fully into the international arms race.

THE IDEOLOGICAL RESPONSE OF THE ARMED FORCES

The new ruling elites tend to emphasize the denationalization and reprivatization of the national economy. As national economic power is returned to the private sector, so is political power. The armed forces see their main historical referent—a socially and economically powerful state—weakening as political power is transferred into the hands of private capital. The state no longer provides an environment for the realization of class domination; the struggle to impose sectoral interests now transpires outside of it. The military has become dislocated within the state, and its response to this institutional anomie is to formulate and stress "super ideologies."[18]

The national security doctrine soon becomes obsolete in the face of new priorities such as the process of accumulation. Consequently, the only military stance that harmonizes with the new national project is the simple pursuit of modernity as an absolute value. In military terms, this has translated into an overemphasis on supremely advanced war technology[19] and a devaluation of nonmilitary ingredients such as political and diplomatic negotiations or international alliances. The most advanced arms and weapons systems are sought by all the armed forces.

This incorporation of technocratic values leads the armed forces to feel that they fill a normative vacuum in responding to the nostalgia for strength that is deeply rooted in the national psyche.[20] Because the majority of Latin American societies have a limited cultural history and because other institutions have not been able to provide the transcendent sense of a historically rooted civilization, these values exercise a special seduction over the armed forces. Although this does not explain the attachment of the armed forces to the interests of the financial sector, perhaps it helps to explain the special nature of Latin American civil-military relations.[21]

In essence, the incapacity of the armed forces to project their traditional corporatist values onto the national plane has led them to update their ideology, redefining military priorities to stress the values of modernity. It is not by chance that this response occurs especially in countries where a political crisis has brought about great social fragmentation. It is in the face of this olympian task of redeeming or providing substantive values to a nation that the armed forces have come to trumpet their "modernity."

Political crises in Latin America have propelled the armed forces to perform a more pronounced and systematic internal political function, generating material and ideological "necessities" that may be satisfied only by incorporating the most technologically sophisticated weaponry. Inasmuch as this massive arms buildup has not been accompanied by a real reduction in troops, one may argue that the drive for modernity responds not to a need to economize on personnel, but rather to some deeper cause.

A NATIONAL MILITARY PROJECT

The military quest to amass great quantities of sophisticated arms has been facilitated by the increased autonomy of the armed forces. The accumulated tensions and contradictions within the nation-state, which result from the attempts of the financial sector to dominate society, converge with the declining capacity of the state to establish hegemony. In the conversion of sectoral interests into "national" projects, the Latin American states have become increasingly paralyzed. They cannot even analyze the causes and social effects of this situation. The states are fragmenting as each branch of government becomes disengaged from the next.

As sectoral interests are increasingly emphasized, conflict pervades state routine. The "general interest" the state had aspired to uphold degenerates into a none-too-coherent aggregate of diverse and at times contradictory interests. The project of class domination becomes a compulsive affirmation of the currently predominating interest, without any attempt at synthesis or even acknowledgment of a broader horizon.

Historically, oligarchic efforts to establish political domination based on agricultural production and exports crystallized in Latin America in state structures that resembled European liberal systems. The balance of powers essential to a real and effective equilibrium of social sectors was dissolved by the hegemony of a single elite. That tendency to pursue political dominance continues, yet in the context of extreme fragmentation, this has resulted in each branch of government claiming dominance, or at least autonomy.

The lack of a true and effective "organic" relationship is obvious in the gap between the different branches of the state, as well as between the state and collective social practice. We thus see, at times, an insurmountable barrier between the executive and the social base of diverse governments. Judicial power moves farther and farther from cultural reality, and its interpretations and sentences grow ever further removed from actual social norms. In the legislature, the great propositions of heroic national destiny have become mere rhetoric and do not capture the sincere concern of the whole nation. Given this chasm between the state and the rest of society, each branch of government pursues its own bureaucratic projects and follows its own interests, ignoring the development of the nation as a whole.

The armed forces have used this new autonomy to define their own institutional ends and provide themselves with the means to achieve these ends—with little concern for broader social considerations. The indiscriminate increase in defense spending and arms purchases on the continent is the best example. The excessive autonomy of the armed forces, which is both a consequence and a cause of diminishing civilian control over the military, finds ultimate fulfillment in both the militarization of the whole of society and in the transformation of the military into a new and valid actor on the national political scene. The cessation of the historic pattern of caudillismo is due not only to the presence of more pronounced institutional interests, nor even to the relatively simple processes of modernization and professionalization of the military. It emerges rather from the overall crisis of the state and the resulting bureaucratic autonomy of the military. As a consequence, the institutional presence of the armed forces in national politics has acquired remarkable force. It cannot be viewed as a transitory condition to be cured by a simple "return to the barracks." The military in Latin America has established itself as a valid interlocutor in the national political game.

Because the autonomy of the armed forces reinforces their position as a national political actor, their utilization by new and emerging class factions does not exhaust their institutional potential. On the contrary, the process of transferring state activities to private hands tends to go against them in the long run. The armed forces therefore seek to perform a corporate function that could eventually protect them from greater civilian control: creating an authoritarian formulation of national goals that must be defended through military means. Instead of defining new social alternatives, the armed forces prefer to adopt a project that already has the support of local and international social forces, and they look primarily for nationalist affirmations. This orientation is notably absent among the new financial factions, which stress the privatization of the economy and all other social activities.

Consequently, the armed forces have sought some special "national project" of their own, one that emphasizes their traditional concern for territorial integrity. An example is the not-so-new program by the

Ecuadoran army of introducing to the native population of the Amazon a combination of military instruction and formal education in the Spanish language. The dispute with Peru over the Amazon region lost in 1942 has been an especially important prop for this program. In the Argentine and Chilean cases, the military has stated a need to create a "general consensus regarding border problems," and has even tried to implement projects that establish active borders in habitually deserted or unpopulated areas. In these cases, the educational integration of native national groups is of particular importance. The creation in Peru of a special office for national mobilization during the Juan Velasco Alvarado military government and the Venezuelan army's attempts to colonize the nation's eastern region are good examples of efforts toward creating "national military projects" through authoritarian means.

These efforts might be relatively harmless in a different political and social context, but given the current situation in Latin America and the global context, these projects become additional stimuli for the international arms race. They have an obvious authoritarian bias, are promoted by military factions, not the whole military institution, and are inefficient. The lack of a national consensus on the territorially centered authoritarian projects compels the involved armed forces to increase their effectiveness by increasing their military might, stock of weapons, and regional deployment. The other armed forces in the country inevitably follow suit, feeding the demand for a higher level of military resources and a greater quantity of arms. The autonomy of the different branches of the state results in the militarization of national goals, supported by greater war capability. The arms buildup in Latin America is thus due to general causes, deeply rooted in the national political crisis.

One aspect of militarization that has special relevance in the arms race is the incipient Latin American arms industry. The development of this industry was foreshadowed by the high military budgets. On the basis of these budgets, new and greater quantities of arms and modern weapons systems were incorporated into Latin American armed forces, and the flood of imports led eventually to the production, usually under foreign license, of arms previously imported. This process either reinforces existing war industries, as in the case of Argentina, or helps to create them, as in Brazil, Chile, Peru, Colombia, and Mexico.[22] The development of an arms industry in Latin America has had several important economic and ideological effects.

One of the arguments used to justify the growing foreign indebtedness of Latin American countries and explain their historically low rates of economic growth has been the constant scarcity of capital resources for development plans and projects.[23] In response to the apparent weakness of internal savings and the relative scarcity of capital, the governments made (and some continue to make) large state investments with international financial support. In a context of growing militarization and increased popularity of nationalism and other chauvinist ideologies, military industries seemed perfect candidates for state investment. Yet the mere existence of these industries now contradicts the "scarcity of national capital resources" stance, for most of these industries are consortia in which national private enterprises somehow find the resources to participate.

This demonstrates an important ideological and economic aspect of military industry, generally concealed behind nationalist affirmations: The industry could be created and has prospered only because of highly unequal, concentrated social and economic structures, and it perpetuates these structures. The distribution of income and all social benefits in Latin America is overwhelmingly unequal, and the existing political structure both reflects and reproduces these inequalities. Where the distribution of wealth is so enormously unsymmetrical, productive investment is restricted to those products consumed by the wealthy sectors of society. This helps to explain the crisis of Latin American industry, with its vast unemployed industrial capacity. The high salaries of workers producing luxury items for the high income sectors contrast with the low wages earned by the majority of industrial workers.[24] Industrial investment in consumer goods for broad social sectors would necessitate structural changes and the deconcentration of income. Without deep internal political changes, or at least substantial alterations in the criteria for assigning resources at a national level, this redirection is unlikely.

It is within this context that the existence of a military industry with so few comparative advantages in war technology may be explained. In Europe and the United States, only those companies with an ongoing process of research and development, characteristic of industrialized areas, can afford to establish and develop a highly profitable military industry. In Latin America the military industry, like all productive Latin American industries, produces luxuries for a privileged sector—in this case, the military.

When the armed forces of a country achieve sufficient autonomy and influence, the adage, "I produce weapons, therefore I exist," serves as a principal justification for the assignment of fiscal resources to military industry. This has happened in all Latin American countries in which there is a weapons industry of some importance. The relative abundance of capital for investment in industry finds a privileged consumer in the armed forces.

Although in some cases military industry represents an important source of hard currency—Brazil exports annually almost US$3 billion in weapons—the industry as a whole is maintained only by the internal market. At the base of the apparent profitability of the military industry is a sector of luxury consumers, and if the internal demand for military industries in Latin America were suppressed, few would survive. The Latin American military industry thus duplicates the economic and ideological function performed by the luxuries goods industry: It conceals true distributive inequalities, while reproducing them on a wide scale. Nationalist chauvinist rhetoric, grandly projecting the complex of values promulgated by the military, hides the true political instabilities and economic limitations of many Latin American countries. The arms race in Latin America is due to political and social causes related to the general crisis of participation in these societies. It is manifested in growing defense budgets and an increasingly diversified and sophisticated military industry.

NOTES

1. See René Villareal, "Problemas y perspectivas del comercio y las finanzas internacionales: Los puntos de vista del Sur," *El Trimestre Económico*, October-December 1981; Ricardo H. Arriazu, "Movimientos internacionales de capitales," *Cuadernos de la CEPAL*, no. 32 (1979); and Alvaro Saieh, "Un análisis sobre la posibilidad de evaluar la solvencia crediticia de los países en desarrollo," *Cuadernos de la CEPAL*, no. 36 (1980).

2. See Carlos Portales and Augusto Varas, "La carrera armamentista en América del Sur," *Mensaje*, January-February 1979; and Augusto Varas, "Relaciones hemisféricas e industria militar en América Latina," *Socialismo y Participación* (Lima), no. 17 (1982).

3. For an analysis of these tendencies in recent times see Augusto Varas, "La reinserción de América Latina en el marco estratégico mundial," *Estudios Internacionales*, October-December 1981.

4. A study of the geopolitical implications of national security doctrines is found in John Child, "Geopolitical Thinking in Latin America," *Latin American Research Review* 14, no. 2 (1979).

5. In this respect see Kenneth D. McRae, *Consociational Democracy: Political Accommodation in Segmented Societies* (Toronto: McClelland & Stewart, 1974); Alberto van Klaveren, "Instituciones consociativas y estabilización democrática: Alternativas para Chile?" CED Document no. 6, 1983.

6. See Augusto Varas, "Las nuevas relaciones de poder en América Latina," *APSI*, July 28-August 10, 1981.

7. The following analysis is based on René Villareal, "Problemas y perspectivas del comercio."

8. Ibid.

9. See Xabier Gorostiaga, *Los banqueros del imperio* (Costa Rica: EDUCA, 1979).

10. Villareal, "Problemas y perspectivas del comercio."

11. See Saieh, "Un análisis."

12. Inter-American Development Bank, *El progreso económico social en América Latina*, reports from 1980 to 1983.

13. See Villareal, "Problemas y perspectivas del comercio," p. 917.

14. For the Argentine case see Roberto Frenkel, "El desarrollo reciente de mercado de capitales en la Argentina," *Desarrollo Económico*, no. 78 (July-September 1980).

15. Alejandro Foxley, *Latin American Experiments in Neo-Conservative Economics* (Berkeley: University of California Press, 1983).

16. For the Chilean case see Jorge Marshall, "Gasto público en Chile," *Estudios* (CIEPLAN), no. 5 (1981).

17. ACDA, *World Military Expenditures and Arms Transfers, 1969–1978* (Washington, D.C.: Government Printing Office, 1980). See also Augusto Varas, "Militarización, armamentismo y gasto militar en Chile, 1973–1981," *Documento de Trabajo* (Santiago: FLACSO, 1982).

18. Celso Furtado, "De la ideología del progreso a la ideología del desarrollo," *Universidad de las Naciones Unidas*, HSDRSCA-725/UNUP-298, 1981.

19. See Peter Lock, "La dinámica armamentista: Punto nodal en las estratégias de desarrollo," *El Día* (Mexico), October 26, 1981, especially the chapter entitled "La carrera armamentista." Significantly, it has been the Chilean army that has modernized Chile's public administration by applying techniques of systemic analysis to the administrative reform and that has promoted the use of the information network. These fall under the charge of a high-ranking official.

20. On problems of culture and the formation of the Latin American nation, see Edelberto Torres-Rivas, "La nación: Problemas teóricos e históricos," in Norbert Lechner, ed., *Estado y política en América Latina* (Mexico City: Siglo XXI, 1981).

21. On ideological relations between military personnel and technocrats, see Guillermo O'Donnell, "Las fuerzas armadas y el estado autoritario del Cono Sur de América Latina," in Lechner, *Estado y política*.

22. Varas, "Relaciones hemisféricas."

23. This perspective supporting relative capital scarcity is associated with the positions of the U.S. government in the 1950s and the current perspective of international financial institutions, which is heavily influenced by the United States. In the first case it was indicated that "The government of the United States considered that the best strategy of development depended on the freeing up of private capital, domestic as well as foreign . . . the role of the public loan became relevant with the creation of the Development Loan Fund and the Inter-American Development Bank." Albert O. Hirschman, "Ideologies of Economic Development in Latin America," in A. O. Hirschman, ed., *Latin American Economic Issues* (New York: Twentieth Century Fund, 1961), p. 39. A more recent focus emphasizing the importance of the mobilization and assignment of capital resources across a capital market completely free of state interferences is found in Barend A. de Vries, "Public Policy and the Private Sector," *Finance and Development* (Washington, D.C.: IMF and World Bank, 1981), pp. 4, 5.

24. According to the World Bank, "whatever the ratio of capital and labor that determines the market, a greater equality of personal incomes can be achieved if the property of private capital and the access to public services were distributed in a more egalitarian fashion . . . the maximization of growth of the GNP implies some measures that benefit all groups." Hollis Chenery et al., *Redistribution with Growth* (Oxford: Oxford University Press for the World Bank and IDS, 1974), pp. 43, 48.

4. The Arms Race in Latin America

At first glance, Latin America may not seem to be a particularly outstanding participant in worldwide arms trade. The total value of Latin American arms imports during 1982 reached US$1.07 billion, accounting for 12.7 percent of total Third World arms imports.[1] But the region's military expenditures in 1982 were 17 percent of the Third World's total, following the Middle East and Far East.[2] This ranking seems to contradict Latin America's geographical and political distance from the areas of greatest strategic interest to developed countries. From World War II until the Malvinas War, no Latin American country had participated in any conflicts involving external powers.

These large figures indicate that the recent buildup of arms in the region is highly significant. Compared to regional performance in the past, the 1980s figures show several new and alarming features. In 1981, Latin American countries spent nearly US$1.4 billion on military imports—a record for the region. Public funds allocated to Latin American armed forces grew in the last ten years from US$9.2 billion to 19.7 billion. Total military expenditures in 1982 were 114 percent higher than in 1972.[3]

The arms race in the region has accelerated both in size of expenditure and in sophistication of equipment. Old inventories of U.S. equipment acquired through military aid programs have been replaced by technologically sophisticated weaponry bought on the international market. Purchases of costly modern missiles and aircraft push up the growth rate in spending, along with the increasing share of arms imports within total military expenditures, which rose to 5.5 percent during 1982 from 4.43 percent in 1973.[4]

This tendency, with its negative effects on social and economic development, is not uncommon among Third World countries. The Latin American countries, however, have completed the process of nation building, unlike most African countries; they have not recently been engaged in any war closely linked to the interests of developed countries; they do not have a monopoly on any scarce strategic resources that might involve them in international disputes or give them control of great currency inflows. Therefore, the recent trend of increased arms expenditure in Latin America compels further research and analysis.

Military spending in Latin America is greatly concentrated among South American countries, which were responsible for over 84.5 percent of total military expenditures in 1982 (see Table 2; figures for Bolivia, Paraguay, and Uruguay are not included in this percentage). In 1982, three countries—Argentina, Brazil, and Chile—absorbed 66.5 percent of total military expenditures in the region, and when Venezuela and Peru are added, these five countries account for 75.4 percent of the region's total arms expenditures. Most Latin American countries have increased their arms imports, although the amount varies from nation to nation (see Table 3). The relative importance of these purchases, however, does not completely explain the expansion of military spending in all the countries. Local production of major weapons has also increased, supplying not only the region but also the international market.[5]

Those features that accompany the accelerated arms buildup in South America—the purchase of major modern weapons from a wide variety of international suppliers, the local production of arms, and the increased consumption of arms by military governments—serve as a guide in endeavoring to understand this phenomenon. Factors related both to the international economic dynamics of arms production and trade and to new national and intraregional processes in the last decade must be taken into account. After considering the political and economic factors involved in the development of arms production, which indicate a change in the supply of weapons, I shall concentrate on the intraregional factors that stimulate the arms race.

DIVERSIFICATION OF ARMS SUPPLIERS

Mirages, Hawker-Hunters, F-5 fighter bombers, Oberon-class submarines, Leanders-class frigates, AMX tanks, Sukhoi bombers, and Exocet, Seacat, and Roland missiles are among the weapons currently possessed by South American countries. They are representative of the major weapons being purchased from a large number of producers.

After World War II South American inventories consisted of second-hand and surplus military hardware. Surplus material was transferred from the United States to the South between 1945 and 1955. Military aircraft totaled 237 units, of which 86.5 percent came from the United Kingdom and 13.5 percent from the United States. Of the 429 units transferred from 1955 to 1965, the United States contributed 53.4 percent; the United Kingdom's participation declined to 17.7 percent; and France ventured 18.6 percent as a new competitor. The United States furnished 49 of the 74 warships transferred to the region from 1945 to 1965.[6]

By the end of the 1960s, the United Kingdom and France had become more prominent as arms suppliers. Sophisticated weapons were made available, although at a higher cost per unit. For example, changing

TABLE 2
Military Expenditures in Latin America, 1973-1982 (In U.S.$ millions at 1980 prices and exchange rates)

	1973	1974	1975	1976	1977	1978	1979	1980	1981	1982
Argentina	2,642	2,691	3,419	3,890	3,979	4,025	3,980	3,942	4,106	9,795
Bolivia	65.9	76.2	104	114	109	118	121	106	141	n.a.
Brazil	2,672	1,873	1,988	2,212	2,017	1,867	1,665	1,303	1,354	1,531
Chile	802	1,196	923	971	1,285	1,443	1,728	2,038	1,761	1,762
Colombia	238	228	253	260	238	220	241	301	269	599
Costa Rica	14	14.5	17.4	23.3	32.7	30.2	32.3	30.9	27.1	n.a.
Cuba	351	366	423	n.a.	909	1,018	1,092	1,053	1,094	1,200
Dominican Republic	76.1	87.5	91.9	100	100	111	127	n.a.	n.a.	n.a.
Ecuador	125	144	176	161	268	204	210	222	215	178
El Salvador	52.8	57.2	51.4	65.3	77.3	80.2	79.8	71.7	101	107
Guatemala	47.1	51.5	71.3	74.7	103	112	116	128	136	n.a.
Honduras	30.2	28.2	33.6	35.5	43.9	56.1	57.3	88	99.8	181
Jamaica	25.9	24.2	30.3	36.8	35.0	n.a.	n.a.	n.a.	n.a.	n.a.
Mexico	569	624	670	752	702	715	796	756	978	1,005
Nicaragua	30.9	39.7	45.6	61	75.7	91.5	60.6	119	146	n.a.
Panama	18.4	19.1	20.5	20.5	n.a.	n.a.	n.a.	n.a.	n.a.	n.a.
Paraguay	44.9	41.7	52.2	54.1	58	60.9	56.3	n.a.	n.a.	n.a.
Peru	533	516	681	772	1,121	851	667	980	857	850
Uruguay	198	238	224	187	200	241	299	258	336	n.a.
Venezuela	618	857	965	704	825	850	848	907	912	920
Total Latin America[a]	9,201	9,226	10,320	11,078	12,279	12,226	12,316	12,631	12,981	19,696

[a]The total includes figures for Guyana, Trinidad and Tobago, and Haiti, not listed here individually.

Source: SIPRI, World Armaments and Disarmament Yearbook 1983 (London: Taylor and Francis, 1983), pp. 165-166.

TABLE 3
Arms Imports by Latin American Countries, 1971-1980
(Figures in constant 1979 US$ millions)

	1971	1972	1973	1974	1975	1976	1977	1978	1979	1980
Argentina	17	98	77	56	38	61	46	401	490	181
Bolivia	8	0	15	7	12	6	5	21	80	36
Brazil	85	98	186	85	129	172	116	228	240	117
Chile	51	16	108	99	25	160	69	65	140	208
Colombia	8	49	62	14	51	0	11	10	20	63
Cuba	51	115	108	85	90	160	116	347	260	235
Ecuador	17	16	31	7	77	110	186	97	180	163
El Salvador	0	0	0	14	6	0	0	5	30	0
Guatemala	17	16	7	0	12	24	5	10	10	9
Honduras	0	0	0	0	0	49	5	5	10	0
Mexico	8	0	7	14	25	24	11	5	10	18
Nicaragua	0	0	0	0	0	0	11	21	5	4
Panama	8	0	0	0	6	0	5	0	0	27
Paraguay	0	0	0	0	0	6	0	10	10	36
Peru	85	131	124	113	155	320	488	336	90	335
Uruguay	17	0	0	0	6	6	23	0	5	27
Venezuela	34	98	139	141	116	73	116	32	30	117
Total Latin America[a]	410	640	869	638	757	1,176	1,220	1,601	1,610	1,612

[a]The total includes figures for Guyana, the Dominican Republic, and Trinidad and Tobago, not listed here individually.

Source: U.S. Arms Control and Disarmament Agency, World Military Expenditures and Arms Transfers 1971-1980 (Washington, D.C.: ACDA, 1983).

from the U.S. F-100 fighter to the F-4 between 1959 and 1969 meant an increase from US$740,000 to US$2.3 million per unit. Replacing the Porpoise-class British submarine with the Oberon-class increased the cost per unit from US$2.2 million to US$3.6 million.[7]

Supplier diversification continued in the 1980s. From 1965 to 1974, the United States remained the largest arms supplier for the region, with 31.9 percent of the region's total purchases, closely followed by France with 18.1 percent. The Soviet Union and the United Kingdom accounted for 14.2 and 11.8 percent of the region's total, respectively.[8] From 1976 to 1980, however, the U.S. share declined to 10.7 percent of total deliveries, while the United Kingdom provided 11.4 percent and West Germany 6.6 percent. France was responsible for 17.6 percent, due primarily to Mirage sales after 1968. For the six largest recipient countries in the region, the United States was the second largest supplier from 1976 to 1980, with 29.4 percent of total deliveries. All other European suppliers combined reached 26.3 percent for the same period. Latin America as a whole buys weapons from the United States, United

Kingdom, France, Switzerland, Italy, West Germany, Austria, Spain, Belgium, and the Netherlands.[9]

Increased expenditures on arms imports have been closely linked to the diversification of arms suppliers during the last decade. The flourishing supply originated with the economic recovery that European countries experienced after World War II, enabling them as technologically sophisticated industrial producers and exporters to penetrate the world arms market. The case of France is perhaps most indicative of this phenomenon. French exports of major weapons increased at an annual rate of 210 percent between 1972 and 1982, compared to the 143.2 percent increase for the world total.[10]

Latin America has been able to take advantage of these developments owing principally to U.S. policies of restraint toward the region and the economic dynamics of capitalist expansion in central industrialized countries. These factors could operate only within the context of détente and the bipolar configuration of the world power structure.

At the beginning of World War II, U.S. military missions were established throughout Latin America to provide logistical aid in the event of an attack by the Axis powers. These bases were later subordinated to U.S. needs during the Cold War. Under U.S. leadership, the region was politically and militarily prepared to prevent or repel an attack by the Soviet Union or Communist bloc countries. The Interamerican Reciprocal Assistance Treaty, signed in Rio de Janeiro in 1947, declared unequivocally that attack on any one of the signatories would be considered as an attack on all. As a result, South American political and military commitment to the United States was assured.

The United States proceeded to equip the region according to the needs it perceived for hemispheric defense. In this process, the countries of the region entered into a number of bilateral military agreements with the United States. The Interamerican Defense Council was established within the frame of the Organization of American States. Along with this institutional support, surplus heavy naval and air weapons were transferred to the region. The United States established itself as the predominant arms supplier to the region by the mid-1960s.

Changes in U.S. strategic interests, defined in response to a new international configuration of military forces,[11] eventually made hemispheric defense an "outmoded concept."[12] The justification for the strategy of hemispheric defense—that is, Soviet attack—became quite unlikely. The usefulness of the weapons being transferred was also questionable. Instead, real threats to U.S. interests in the region were seen as more likely to arise from within continental borders. The poverty and social and economic frustrations of the majority of Latin Americans generated anti-American sentiment in the region, which was said to feed internal communist subversion. Thus, the externally oriented defense strategy was shifted to an internal one. Hemispheric defense was replaced by a policy of security and development, and development was equated with the capitalist modernization of the region. The Alliance for Progress became the channel to achieve these ends. Due to concerns over security, emphasis was placed on internal repression and control rather than on preparing for external warfare.

This shift had at least two important consequences. First, armies were no longer viewed as a reserve force to be deployed only in the case of external aggression. Instead, they were given an important role in controlling internal subversion. During John F. Kennedy's administration, Secretary of Defense Robert MacNamara stressed "the essential role of the Latin American military as a stabilizing force."[13] Secondly, programs of military assistance were altered. The proportion of assistance devoted to training the military in counterinsurgency warfare was increased to roughly double the world total. The share of military assistance for training programs, which averaged 8 percent from 1950 to 1964, had doubled by 1967.[14] Also, new types of weapons suited to counterinsurgency warfare were made available to the region. The transfer of lighter and cheaper weaponry in accordance with the new security priorities was also meant to stimulate investment and development, which had often suffered when funds were diverted to costly weapons programs. This became another major goal of U.S. military policy toward the region.

The political factors that constrain and determine military policies and arms transfers explain the position of the United States as the single main supplier of weapons tailored to counterinsurgency. In the 1950s the United States supplied 94.5 percent of Latin American purchases of counterinsurgency weapons, 81 percent during the 1960s, and a still impressive 65 percent from 1970 to 1972.[15] Political factors affecting the policies of arms transfers originated not only from strategic definitions and investment priorities, but also from U.S. interests in maintaining a military balance between regions. However, the pursuit of these goals often conflicted with restrictions on transfers established by the executive branch and by Congress. The flexibility needed to implement global policies occasionally led U.S. presidents to bypass congressional rules and operate instead through secret programs. Agreements between the U.S. Department of Defense and the Export-Import Bank allowed the financing of arms transfers through "Country X Loans" without informing Congress.[16] Congress reacted with closer control and restrictions.

Due to these restrictions, the countries of Latin America came to perceive the United States as an uncertain arms supplier. Total military deliveries from the United States to Latin America declined from US$421 million between 1963 and 1967 to US$316 million between 1968 and 1972. Furthermore, the composition of military deliveries shifted as changes in the military aid program increased the portion dedicated to U.S. foreign military sales. From 1963 to 1967, foreign military sales accounted for 36 percent of total assistance; from 1968 to 1978 the figure was 82.6 percent.[17] In the 1968–1972 period no Latin American orders for destroyers, submarines, tanks, or fighting aircraft were received by the United States.[18] Perhaps the most significant indicator of U.S. decline as chief arms supplier to the region was Peru's 1968 decision to purchase French Mirage 5s and British Canberra bombers after the United States refused to sell F-5 fighters. The Peruvian example was subsequently followed by Argentina, Brazil, Colombia, and Venezuela.

Faced with the potential alienation of the region's armed forces, the United States modified its arms transfer policy again. The *Rockefeller Report* explicitly emphasized regional resentment against U.S. restrictions and stated the necessity of being congenial with major weapons purchasers. This report influenced the Richard Nixon and Gerald Ford administrations' policies on this issue.[19] Sales of modern equipment were resumed in the 1970s, but new political restrictions were placed on arms transfers during the Jimmy Carter administration, reinforcing the view that the United States is a difficult and not quite reliable supplier. Besides the formal legal restrictions, other difficulties have resulted from the lack of coordination between the U.S. public and private sectors. Such is not the case with the aggressive, pragmatic, and state-supported European arms merchants.

The decline of the United States as a regional arms supplier has not affected its political influence, even in the military sphere. Political factors have predominated over economic concerns in military aid packages, as can be seen in the constant support of training programs. In fiscal year 1978 the Carter administration requested US$8.5 million for Latin America under the International Military Education and Training (IMET) program. This was 24 percent of the total requested for all forms of military aid.[20] Furthermore, although the proposed foreign military sales financing to American republics for fiscal year 1979 was 18.6 percent less than the average for 1977–1978 and proposed funds for military assistance programs were 70.8 percent less, funds requested for military education and training were 14.7 percent higher for 1979.[21] The number of students trained under the IMET program has decreased for many countries in the region, increased for others. Some, including Brazil, Uruguay, and Chile, had no trainees whatsoever in 1977. Other major arms purchasers, such as Argentina and Colombia, had almost the same number of trainees in 1977 as during the 1970–1976 period—in some cases more. The number of trainees from Ecuador and Peru were, respectively, 64 percent and 92 percent higher in 1977 than in the period from 1970 to 1976.[22]

The recent decline in U.S. domestic demand has resulted in idle capacity in the aircraft industry and increased pressure for expanded exports,[23] which may influence U.S. policy on arms transfers to Latin America. The Reagan administration has pursued a new policy toward the region, emphasizing close relations with the military, an interest in their special ability to maintain stability in the region, and a willingness to satisfy their demands for weapons. Yet because of the proliferation of many competing suppliers, the capacity of the United States to control Latin American purchases has declined.

PRESSURE TO EXPAND ARMS EXPORTS

Increasing arms exports has become a popular solution for the economic crises of central capitalist countries suffering from increased oil prices and shortfalls in their balance of payments. During the recent world economic recession, which reached its peak in 1973, major arms producers increased their arms exports. Although the value of U.S. and West German exports in 1973 fell by 11.7 percent and 86 percent respectively relative to their 1970–1972 average, British exports did not vary, and French and Italian exports grew by 94 percent and 24 percent. Taken together, these five countries' exports grew by 6 percent in 1973 with respect to the average of the previous three years. Thereafter, total exports of the three main suppliers to the Third World—the United States, the United Kingdom, and France—were 208 percent, 97 percent, and 156 percent higher during the 1974–1977 period than the 1970–1972 period. Italian exports increased by 191 percent and West German exports by 481 percent as those countries became major arms suppliers. The total value of arms exports by these five countries to the Third World was, as an average, 168 percent higher from 1974 to 1977 than in 1973.[24]

The increase in arms exports as part of economic recovery is an indicator of the economic importance of overall military expenditures. For example, allocations to the U.S. Department of Defense grew significantly in 1965–1967, but then stagnated until 1974. Growth was resumed with the economic recession. Persistent economic stagnation inspired an increase in military spending to reinforce other measures, such as social expenditure, that were used to reactivate the economy.[25]

Data show that increased arms exports have been an important resource for central capitalist countries in times of economic crisis. However, from a global point of view, relying on an increase of arms exports may not have the desired effect of countering balance-of-payment difficulties. The impact of arms exports on the balance of payments may be offset by reductions of capital equipment purchases and other non-military exports.[26] This could explain the large deficit in the U.S. commercial balance during 1983.

Moreover, in the early 1970s none of the major arms suppliers were largely dependent upon arms exports. In none of these capitalist countries did arms exports account for more than 0.4 percent of its gross national product (GNP) in 1975.[27] Here, the United States should be considered separately from Europe. While U.S. total exports represented 7.2 percent of its GNP in 1975, those of France and Britain were almost 15 percent. However, U.S. military exports were 4.5 percent of total exports; the French and British figures were no higher than 0.9 percent.[28] Although none of these countries can be said to be heavily dependent upon arms exports, individual industries and corporations within each country certainly are.

Among those British enterprises that account for half of that nation's total arms exports, weapons account for 31 percent of total sales.[29] The dependency of the British shipbuilding industry on military exports rose from 10 percent in 1971 to 38 percent in 1974.[30] In France, arms exports rose by more than 20 percent annually between 1960 and 1971, accounting for more than 20 percent of that nation's defense production in 1970. Exports from the French aerospace industry have increased threefold since the 1960s, with the share of exports in total production of this industry rising from 25 percent in 1960 to over 70 percent in 1970.[31] Exports from the French naval industry rose from 3 to 14 percent of total production from 1971 to 1974.[32] In the United States, the aircraft industry's share of military exports is 30 percent smaller than that of France and Britain. The increase in military business from foreign sources for U.S. arms manufacturers has meant, however, that the ten corporations responsible for the largest foreign military sales (FMS) contracts received an average of 30.5 percent of their total fiscal year 1976 military contracts from foreign countries. The largest FMS contractor during 1976—Northrop—received 87 percent of its military contracts from foreign countries. Other top corporations also saw considerable increases in their foreign sales for 1976.[33]

The increasing number of industries and corporations moving into the arms business in central capitalist countries indicates that this is a main channel for economic expansion. From the viewpoint of suppliers, the expansion of exports emphasizes the logic of accumulation in the arms industries of capitalist exporting countries. The pressure to export arms from military industries is particularly strong in Europe. Increasing technological complexity and the need to shorten production time in order to reduce costs and to facilitate recovery of expenses have encouraged further military research and development. For the European arms industries, domestic demand is insufficient to absorb the amount of production required to justify investments. French and British governments claim that their aerospace industries must export at least half their output in order to survive.[34] By comparison, U.S. arms development is mainly oriented toward providing domestic military needs. Exporting is secondary.[35]

In Europe, exporting has become an object of deliberate and aggressive policies. The case of France is particularly indicative of market penetration. France has acquired all the markets orphaned by the political restrictions of other suppliers. France became a major supplier to South Africa after the British embargo in 1964, and to Pakistan after the U.S. embargo to India and Pakistan in 1965. France also received orders from Greece for major weapons after the U.S. embargo, and provided Portugal with counterinsurgency (COIN) weapons to be used in Africa. In South

America, France began to supply the Mirage to several countries, including Pinochet's Chile, after the United States refused sales in 1968 and in the 1970s.[36]

European countries have been completely pragmatic in their export policies, placing few political restrictions on arms sales. They also attract buyers by their efforts to consider foreign buyers' needs in designing major weapons. As part of this orientation, they have adapted multiple-task arms for sophisticated and unsophisticated uses. Examples are the French Mirage 3 and Mirage 5 and the Anglo-French produced Jaguar. Europe's major arms exporting countries have also demonstrated greater coordination between private and public sectors. Nationalization has in effect allowed state subsidies of arms industries. Two-thirds of British arms production and trade is in the hands of the government. The nationalization of the French Dassault aerospace industry is another example of this trend.

This strategy appears in the United States in the form of collaborative government-producer relations.[37] The state is interested in promoting military sales abroad because this increases domestic employment, preserves technological expertise, and supports domestic arms production. Military sales have also contributed to the expansion of nonmilitary trade and investment. "It is common for arms sales and military assistance to form part of a wider 'package,' including trade and investment agreements on political accords."[38]

In France, arms agreements have also been part of larger commercial agreements. When Argentina signed the AMX-13 deal with France for the assembly of thirty tanks in Argentina, the government-owned Régie Nationale des Usines Renault acquired a controlling interest in the firm that would produce the tanks in Argentina.[39] France also sold an air-traffic control system for US$60 million to Brazil, seemingly in continuation of the Mirage sales.[40] The French sales of Mirage planes to Chile were accompanied by other bilateral agreements.

The entrance of aggressive competitors into the arms market has transformed the ownership structure and the production of arms-exporting corporations.[41] Their mergers, centralization, and integration influence the arms-purchasing process among Latin American countries, reinforcing European pressures to export while also enticing some South American countries to produce and export arms themselves. This has increased the complexity of the regional arms race.

There are many examples of the internationalization of arms production through joint ventures, coproduction, and licencing. These forms of internationalization are motivated by increasing production costs and have facilitated expansion of production, recovery of costs, and securing of key markets. The tendency is particularly notable among central capitalist countries. The Spanish production of labor-intensive parts for Northrop's F-5 allowed a considerable saving and is a good example of the rationale for internationalization.

Export campaigns, changes within the arms industry, and the internationalization of arms production "are all potential means of overcoming
the structural crisis in the arms economies of major capitalist countries.
. . . From this point of view growing militarization of the Third World
is a reflection of the armament dynamic and production problems of
developed countries."[42]

From the suppliers' viewpoint, the rationality of internationalization
seems clear in Latin America. Securing a market and overcoming
competition within it are chief motives for coproducing or licencing in
the region. The majority of aircraft builders admit that in order to sell
to Brazil, for example, some sort of coproduction arrangements are
necessary.[43] Cheap labor is of equal importance: "Helicopters and light
COIN aircraft are now manufactured in Colombia, Argentina, Brazil
and Taiwan, in each case at lower cost than by the U.S. licenser. The
lion's share of value added regularly remains, however, in the United
States where the more complicated components of these products are
made." Other advantages are offered "by infrastructure investment,
cheap credit and taxing terms, and the repression of the work force
guaranteed by local governments."[44] There is no ambiguity in this regard
from the countries in the region. As the director of the War Material
Industry of Brazil (IMBEL), General Calderari, stated, "Brazil can offer
a guarantee of political tranquility, a versatile labor force that is much
cheaper than in Europe, and an industrial base that has already attained
a high degree of development."[45]

Coproduction and licencing agreements are spreading rapidly throughout Latin America, particularly with Brazilian and Argentinian companies.
A brief outline of regional arms production will substantiate this assertion.
Brazil, through Empresa Brasileira de Aeronautica (EMBRAER), manufactures certain components for the F-5E as part of an agreement for
purchasing F-5s.[46] Under licence and coproduction agreements with
Italian Aermacchi, EMBRAER assembled training COIN Xavantes, some
of which have already been delivered. Lama helicopters produced under
French licence and Roland French-German surface-to-air missiles (SAMs)
are also being assembled. Aerospatiale of France has purchased a minority
interest in Helibras, the Brazilian helicopter manufacturer. EMBRAER
light planes of various types have already been sold under licence from
the United States, and German COBRA antitank missiles went into
production in Brazil in 1975. British Niteroi destroyers have been in
production since 1972; and Italy's Oto Melara has joined two Brazilian
corporations in building an arms production complex in Pernambuco.[47]
Brazil is also producing many domestically designed heavy weapons.
Uirapuru and Universal trainers were designed during the 1960s. Also,
Bandeirante light transports have been ordered, many by other Latin
American countries. In addition to the four types of aircraft being
produced, armored vehicles, submarines, patrol boats, missiles, and
turbojet engines are either under development or already in the process
of assembly.

Argentina, with licences from U.S. corporations, has built Cessna and other planes. Twenty out of 120 planned Hughes Model-500 helicopters have already been built. The share of components in these helicopters produced domestically will rise from 22 percent in 1977 to 50 percent in 1982.[48] Other weapons are also being built with European licences: fast missile boats, destroyers, and frigates. Production of the domestically designed Pucará COIN combat aircraft began in 1977, and 8 had been produced by 1979. Other jet attack and trainer planes, helicopters, and survey ships are in production. French AMX tanks and Swiss Mowag armored vehicles have also been assembled under coproduction agreements since 1968.[49]

Brazil and Argentina are by far the largest arms producers in the region, but other countries are joining them. Colombia has been assembling Cessna planes since 1972. Peru is producing modified Lupo guided missile frigates, has built Parina tankers and large patrol crafts, and has expressed interest in constructing helicopters. Peru and Venezuela may receive Israeli licences, although a similar licence for Ecuador was vetoed in 1977 by the United States. Venezuela plans to construct three major shipyards and has been building coastal patrol craft since 1974 under Italian licence.

Several factors need to be considered in order to interpret this process correctly. In the majority of cases, no prized technology was transferred through coproduction or licencing. Instead, old "surplus" technology was transferred and then traded among peripheral or semiperipheral countries. This demonstrates the subordinate and dependent integration of Latin America into the structure of international capitalist arms production. Coproduction and licencing in the region have lowered costs, extended the use of outmoded technology, and assured a market for products, as the coproducer or licenced country buys or exports products within the region or to other underdeveloped countries. Thus, through increasing internationalization, arms companies alleviate their cost problems while also securing markets that otherwise would be difficult to enter.

Intraregional arms trade adds to the complexity of the Latin American arms trade. Some countries—Brazil and Argentina—are both recipients and suppliers. Brazilian exports reached US$47 million between 1970 and 1976. Of this total, 98 percent went to other countries within Latin America and the rest to sub-Saharan Africa. As already noted, in 1983 Brazilian weapon exports totaled US$2 billion, and included the sale of armored personnel carriers to Iraq, Qatar, and Libya. In the mid-1970s, Argentina exported US$3.5 million in weapons to other countries in Latin America, particularly Bolivia, Paraguay, and Peru.[50]

The increased production and export of Brazilian arms is a form of dependent capitalist industrial expansion and brings industrialists into the lucrative arms business. Brazil has managed to gather approximately fifty of its biggest suppliers of vehicle parts into a program to produce and export a variety of aircraft parts and engines.[51] EMBRAER, Brazil's largest aircraft producer, is 49 percent privately owned; Volkswagen do Brasil is the major private shareholder.[52] Thus, regional integration into internationalized arms production has meant the restructuring of productive capacity in arms-producing countries.

Most of the major coproducers and licencers in Latin America are not from the United States, but from Europe—particularly Italy, France, Great Britain, and West Germany. Power plants for indigenously designed weapons also come mainly from France, Canada, and West Germany, although U.S. participation is relatively greater here. This coincides with world patterns in the origin of licences. Whereas U.S. firms have six licenced production projects in peripheral countries, West European firms have seventeen.[53] The sphere of internationalized arms production thus illustrates the swift emergence of European competitors in their search for markets and lower costs.

NEW INTERNATIONAL CONDITIONS

The possibilities for effective market penetration in the region by new competitors were enhanced by détente between world superpowers. After World War II, the world was divided into two main spheres of influence, capitalist and socialist. U.S. political, economic, and military hegemony over the capitalist sphere paralleled the powerful role of the Soviet Union in the socialist sphere. This configuration of power shaped international relations according to the main political confrontations between the two poles. Power disputes between the United States and the Soviet Union created a bipolar orientation in international relations, with the consequent risk of global confrontation as both sides maintained and spurred the race in military developments. This bipolar configuration is embodied in several treaties. The Soviet Union formalized its status as a major power through the Warsaw Treaty; the United States clearly dominates in the North Atlantic Treaty Organization and the Southeast Asian Treaty Organization, as well as in the Interamerican Reciprocal Assistance Treaty.

One of the most striking features of this bipolar configuration was its cohesion despite the diversity within each bloc. This situation began to change when, due to their nuclear capability and to the enormous military power accumulated on both sides, the imperative of avoiding a global confrontation became clear. The United States and the Soviet Union initiated a process to alleviate international tensions, encouraged by other nations who saw their own existence endangered. This process weakened the internal cohesion of each bloc, as did concurrent economic and political developments, particularly though not exclusively within the capitalist bloc.

Détente has been favored not only by socialist countries, but also within the international communist movement. This is important because some Communist parties exert considerable influence on the national politics of certain Western European countries and account for their decreased linkage to the Soviet bloc. However, our primary interest here is in the effects of détente and political diversity in the capitalist camp, as Latin America has been more involved in its dynamics.

Diversity and the lack of cohesion are demonstrated on several fronts. European and Japanese economic development have caused problems in the world capitalist economic order and contributed to the end of an international monetary system based on the U.S. dollar. On the military front, France has questioned NATO, and events in Greece and Turkey have caused open conflict among allies. The development of European military industry indicates a trend toward a new multipolar configuration of world order. Political opportunities are found in the less rigid international patterns of détente, and allow the projection of industrial capacity into effective widespread export policies and market penetration.

Increased flexibility in international relations has also made a degree of peaceful interbloc penetration possible. Soviet sales to Cuba and Peru are examples. Greater independence in international relations is clear in the West German agreement to build nuclear facilities in Brazil at the risk of displeasing its major allies.[54] Even the U.S. move to decrease its role as an arms supplier in Latin America can be viewed as a consequence of détente. Abating international tension has decreased the need to integrate Latin America into the U.S. defense system. In this sense, a reduction in military aid due to political considerations and an increase in commercial sales of weapons are quite understandable.[55] As transfers of U.S. military goods shifted from aid programs to commercial sales, other difficulties arose. Competition became a factor because the United States had lost political control over arms transfers and was no longer able to impede diversification of political influence or arms supply.

Diversification of political influence is not easily measured. It cannot be stated, for example, that the political influence the United States lost owing to restrictions on arms transfers is precisely counterbalanced by the increased influence of new suppliers. Nonetheless, changes in political influence are related. Brazil has closer ties with West Germany at present because of West German involvement in Brazilian nuclear development. In the process of developing into a semiperipheral exporting country, Brazil has increased its independence and expanded its influence in certain African countries. Peruvian purchases from noncapitalist countries have also encouraged a degree of independence from particular suppliers, although this is circumscribed by the need for foreign currency. The possibilities for acquiring political influence are enormous and arise from economic and technological dependency on a variety of suppliers, from coproducers and licencers to sellers of finished products.

Decreased U.S. strategic and military concerns in the region before the Malvinas crisis also made room for diverse forms of political influence.

As U.S. security became a matter of global weapons systems, the particular strength of a limited region seemed less vital. These new strategic considerations led to different conceptions of security, such as the "coalition of security,"[56] characterized by greater fluidity and a de-emphasis on regional alliances.

The basis of diversification of political influence in the context of détente should be sought in the crisis of hegemony within the Western world. This crisis emerges from the loss of a monolithic identity due to the transnational pursuit of national interests. This transnational approach is particularly evident in the arms business, but is much broader and deeper. The factors underlying this process may be found in the logic of international capitalist expansion.

FACTORS UNDERLYING THE DEMAND FOR ARMS IN LATIN AMERICA

Détente is a good starting point for identifying and analyzing sources of Latin American demand for major weapons. While détente allowed the expansion of arms exports to the region, it also increased actual demand. This is related both to Latin America's position within the international order and to the intraregional situation. The former enables regional acceptance of diversified suppliers; the latter stimulates the demand for weapons. Another factor reinforcing the arms buildup is the type of military government that has become widespread within the region.

From World War II through the mid-1960s, commitment to hemispheric unity under U.S. leadership was unequivocal. With subsequent events, however, hemispheric cohesion has come to be seen as an outmoded concept. Together with the tensions produced by U.S. restrictions on arms transfers, growing economic and political differences between the United States and Latin America became acute. Nonsymmetrical economic relations between these neighbors frustrated Latin American nations and led to regional attempts to countervail inequality through a political restructuring of economic relations. Among these efforts, an attempt was made to alter the plane of dialogue between the United States and Latin American countries. Rather than the customary country by country discussions, Latin America sought to be identified as a single entity. This was clear in the 1969 Viña del Mar meeting of Latin American secretaries of foreign affairs, which established the Latin American Economic System (SELA). By then, the ineffectiveness of inter-American political bodies, such as the Organization of American States, in shaping hemispheric relations according to the needs of Latin America was widely recognized.

In addition, poverty and exploitation of the masses made structural changes imperative. Political movements with anti-imperialist platforms gained influence. As international relations shifted from a bipolar to a multipolar configuration and world tensions diminished with détente, opportunities arose for reform movements to enter government. The Peruvian, Ecuadorian, and Venezuelan governments nationalized some of their copper and all of their oil plants. Salvador Allende's Popular Unity government expropriated a number of U.S.-owned companies; Bolivia experienced a series of brief anti-imperialist governments. The Alejandro Lanusse government in Argentina distanced itself from ideology, while contributing to the emergence of the Héctor Cámpora–Juan Perón government and the expansion of Argentine-Soviet economic relations.

All these trends led to greater political independence from the United States and the possibility of greater autonomy in international relations. Several countries refused to continue the isolation of Cuba. Some Andean countries and even Argentina, which had contributed two ships to the blockade against Cuba only a few years before, reestablished diplomatic relations with Cuba in the 1960s and 1970s. By then many Latin American countries had also commenced diplomatic and commercial relations with the Soviet Union and Eastern European countries. In the economic realm, there were joint efforts to promote autonomous regional development, such as the Andean Pact and SELA.

This trend of relaxed hemispheric ties was completed by specific developments in the military field. The close ties between the U.S. and Latin American armed forces that had been established by the Interamerican Reciprocal Assistance Treaty (Rio Treaty) and military assistance programs began to falter in response not only to U.S. restrictions but also to internal developments within the region. The Rio Treaty preventing Soviet or other extracontinental "aggression" was never utilized as such. It was invoked by the United States to legitimate its policies of intervention—for example, its invasion of the Dominican Republic in 1965—but the treaty was never usefully invoked to impede intraregional aggression. This distorted use of inter-American organizations or treaties eroded the ability of the United States to assert its counterinsurgency programs, as shown by the unfruitful attempt to build a so-called Interamerican Peace Force. The United States could no longer manage the Southern military establishment as its own in the arms trade business.

Some factions in the military became aware of the growth of national popular movements and of changes in international relations. At the Tenth Conference of American Armies (1973) there were ideological confrontations over the armed forces' conceptions of the military's role and identity. Shifting from their previous Cold War and bipolar perspective, the Argentine and Peruvian armies (Peru having an anti-imperialist government) stressed the need to define external aggression in a wide sense, to include not only actual invasion, but also economic and political subordination. Additionally, national sovereignty was said to be threatened by the expansion of multinational companies and by the unequal distribution of internal wealth.[57]

Although this conception did not prevail in the long run, high-ranking military personnel who subsequently came to power, sometimes as heads of state, could not simply ignore it. Initial hemispheric cohesion had been broken, and the military doctrines that later tried to recuperate the ideological climate of the Cold War and a close relationship with the United States were based on wishful thinking. A political hiatus between the U.S. and Latin American militaries and a lack of cohesion within the region became characteristic. Although basic ideologies were still shared and hemispheric organizations and common military activities continued, these were not sufficient to maintain the old links. When the United States tied military aid to respect for human rights, Brazil decided to refuse aid rather than accept the restrictions.

Human rights violations motivated cuts in U.S. military aid to several other countries in Latin America. Initiatives to limit aid proceeded from both the U.S. executive branch and Congress. As a result, Latin America has moved away from U.S. military leadership, replacing it with diverse codes of conduct from country to country. This pattern is easily perceived in military establishments that can assert their own goals because they also control the government. The Brazilian military emphasizes development of military industry and export within the framework of a consolidated internal domination; the Uruguayan, Bolivian, and Chilean militaries concentrate on controlling internal affairs and remain more dependent on external arms purchases. What had been a relatively balanced relationship shifted toward a supplier-recipient relationship within the continent. Argentina is modestly following Brazil; Peru remains the only country with purchases from the socialist bloc.

The weakening of hemispheric ties and the greater independence of movement within the international scene[58] will probably continue and result in access to an even wider variety of arms suppliers.

INTRAREGIONAL CONFLICTS

Paradoxically, the relaxation of international tension has given rise to new tensions within Latin America that may lead to armed conflict. The possibility of such conflicts has contributed greatly to the acceleration of the arms race. In the framework of the previous hemispheric cohesion, old rivalries and frontier problems between Latin American countries were dormant, but once this cohesion dissolved old issues were reactivated, compounded by new conflicts produced by more recent intraregional changes. Thus, the complexity of potential intraregional conflict has increased. The economic growth of some Latin American countries has led them to develop economic areas in border regions. The resulting conflicts of interest exacerbate old unresolved border disputes. Border problems have historically been a main cause of wars in the region. This potential conflict situation is complicated by the process of nation building and by disputes over areas that have not yet been economically integrated. A brief summary of the main areas of potential conflict will suffice to show their complexity and to demonstrate how they stimulate the regional arms race.

Marshalling the enormous hydroelectric resources contained in the Cuenca del Plata zone has been a difficult problem for Argentina and Brazil, and involves Paraguay as well. The first two nations, by far the largest countries and economic powers in Latin America, have a great economic interest in the area. The future industrial development of both Buenos Aires and São Paulo depends largely on the exploitation of energy resources from this zone. There has been considerable disagreement over the courses international rivers will follow, as this entails enormous investments in and control over dams. Such disputes have fed military spending in both countries and have been used to justify some of the largest arms purchases in the region's history.

Another major area of dispute has been between Chile and Argentina, over the Beagle Channel. Arguments over the sovereignty of three islands have expanded to the wider issue of sea jurisdiction. Argentina's refusal to accept Britain's arbitration exacerbated the dispute, and the two countries came close to armed conflict. Although resources in the area are as yet unknown, the southern portal of the Atlantic Ocean and entrances to Antartica are thought to be of considerable future geopolitical and geoeconomic importance. This rivalry has also stimulated arms purchases by the two countries, particularly of naval materiel. The recent treaty signed by Argentina and Chile committing both countries to a peaceful settlement of this controversy, combined with the altered military policy of the new democratic government in Argentina, may diminish pressure on their military budgets.

Implicit alliances and open friendships between countries can be understood in terms of the many opportunities for conflict in the region. Chile's dispute with Argentina encouraged the former to build its friendship with Brazil, a rival of Argentina. Brazil exports arms to Chile, but not to Argentina. In turn, Argentina exports no arms to either Brazil or Chile. Instead, Argentina is selling arms to Bolivia and Peru, the other two protagonists in potential conflict with Chile.

The rivalry between Chile and Peru began with Chile's acquisition of rich mineral resources and vast territories as a result of the Pacific War a century ago. The dispute is complicated by Bolivian claims to a sovereign coast. Bolivia has been landlocked since the Pacific War, and the right to sea access has become a national rallying cry. Chile's comparative inferiority in major weapons, particularly in armored vehicles and aircraft, has led Chile to seek Brazilian friendship. However, Brazil's chances of access to the Pacific Ocean lie more in its friendship with Bolivia. Bolivia has been entirely flexible in its alliances, willing to participate in any relationship that may lead to possession of an outlet to the sea. Chile also desires friendship with Ecuador, another nation in conflict with Peru. A militarily dependent Chile itself exported arms valued at US$500,000 to Ecuador during 1970–1976.

Ecuadorian military inferiority vis-à-vis Peru is undeniable, but Ecuador's recent purchases of major weapons, mainly aircraft, have nonetheless transformed this country into a risk that Peru cannot ignore. Peruvian-Ecuadorian conflict dates from the Peruvian occupation of Ecuadorian territory during the 1942 war. The disputed Amazon region is rich in natural and energy resources. Ecuadorian persistence in reaching a solution based on "justice and equity" may keep this conflict alive for a long time.[59] Other longstanding conflicts are those between Colombia and Nicaragua over the San Andres Islands and, more important, between Colombia and Venezuela over the oil-rich zone of the Gulf of Venezuela.

The swift emergence or reemergence of intraregional disputes caused by unresolved border problems and by conflicts over zones crucial to economic expansion have altered the intraregional balance and stimulated the arms race in Latin America.[60] Neither the widening of the international supply of arms, however, nor the existence of these disputes completely explains the increased purchases of major weapons in the region. The identity and perspectives of the decision-makers must also be considered. In the majority of Latin American countries, these actors are military institutions with a particular set of doctrines.

MILITARY DOCTRINES

The rate of military spending in Latin America has accelerated whenever the military takes control of the government. Regardless of the circumstances of intraregional problems, the military has invariably responded by increasing arms purchases.[61] The old military proverb, *si vis pacem para bellum* (if you desire peace, prepare for war), is a good introduction to the prevailing doctrine of national security.

The origin and specific content of military doctrines varies from country to country depending on historical factors and on the specific geographic conditions of national settlement. Common to all Latin American miitaries, however, is the influence of European doctrines. This began with the establishment of armed forces and continued with their professionalization under the tutelage of European missions. The U.S. military added its own ideological influence through joint activities, education, and training programs. The common doctrinal features that do exist among the armed forces of the region reinforce a predilection toward arms acquisitions.

A concept of the military as having total strength and expertise is of considerable use for legitimating authoritarian right-wing military governments. The emergence of this type of government in alliance with the forces of national and international financial sectors tends to overemphasize military preparedness, as already described. In the underdeveloped dependent countries of Latin America, which hardly control even their own development, doctrines of national security exaggerate the importance of defense and the needs of the military. National security doctrines operating through public policies reinforce military power and allocate economic resources in case of a warlike emergency.

Military emphasis on this development of "national power" and the lack of civil representation in national planning or defense affairs (allowing unlimited secrecy) contribute to a particular understanding of intraregional relations that encourages accelerated arms expenditures. Military exaltation of patriotic symbols, generally linked to past wars with bordering countries, stimulates a climate of martial readiness among the population, at times creating a sort of chauvinistic mobilization. Military control of governments in the region must therefore be considered a key factor in the escalation of the arms race.

This analysis has not attempted to rank the different elements that influence the arms race in Latin America. However, the contributing factors identified above indicate why purchases of major weapons have been increasing and how such purchases have become possible. Arms sellers need arms buyers, and buyers need strong motives for purchasing weapons beyond being "tempted" by an attractive and readily available supply.[62] The intraregional situation favors the procurement of arms, as does the governing military's conception of national development within the intraregional context. The latter interpretation, which arises largely from doctrines of national security, identifies national development with the increase of "national power"—whose main components are arms and defense establishments. The generalized influence of military governments in Latin America, particularly in the framework of renewed rivalries and conflicts of interest within the continent, persistently and reciprocally stimulate arms acquisitions.

NOTES

This chapter is a revised and updated version of Augusto Varas, Carlos Portales, and Felipe Agüero, "National and International Dynamics of South American Armamentism," *Current Research on Peace and Violence*, no. 1 (1980).

1. Stockholm International Peace Research Institute (SIPRI), *World Armaments and Disarmament Yearbook 1983* (hereafter referred to as *SIPRI Yearbook 1983*) (London: Taylor and Francis, 1983), pp. 165–166.

2. Ibid., pp. 290–291.

3. Figures elaborated from data provided in *SIPRI Yearbook 1983*.

4. Ibid. See also Richard F. Grimmett, "Trends in Conventional Arms Transfers to the Third World by Major Supplier, 1976–1983," Congressional Research Service, Report no. 84-82 F, May 7, 1984.

5. Paraguay, Peru, Bolivia, Chile, and Uruguay have purchased arms of local production in Brazil and Argentina. Togo in sub-Saharan Africa and countries of the Middle and Far East have been recipients outside the region for Brazilian, Argentinian, and Chilean exports.

6. John L. Sutton and Geoffrey Kemp, "Arms to Developing Countries: 1945–1965," *Adelphi Papers*, October 1966.

7. Ulrich Albrecht, "The Cost of Armamentism," *Journal of Peace Research,* no. 3 (1973), and "Armament and Inflation," *Instant Research on Peace and Violence,* no. 3 (1974).

8. See Arms Control and Disarmament Agency (ACDA), *World Military Expenditures and Arms Transfers, 1965–1974* (Washington, D.C.: Government Printing Office, 1976).

9. ACDA, *World Military Expenditures and Arms Transfers, 1976–1980* (Washington, D.C.: Government Printing Office, 1983).

10. *SIPRI Yearbook 1983,* p. 292.

11. Peter Althaus, "La evolución de la doctrina militar norteamericana después de 1945," *Memorial del Ejército de Chile,* no. 356 (July-August 1970).

12. SIPRI, *The Arms Trade with the Third World* (Harmondsworth, Eng.: Penguin Books, 1975), p. 273.

13. Ibid.

14. Ibid.

15. Data taken from ibid., p. 272.

16. Ibid., p. 74.

17. L. Einaudi, H. Heymann, Jr., D. Ronfeldt, and C. Sereseres,"Transferencia de armas a Latinoamérica: Hacia una política de respeto mutuo," in CIDE, *La dependencia militar latinoamericana* (Mexico), no. 4 (1978), p. 334.

18. Ibid., p. 333.

19. Nelson A. Rockefeller, *The Rockefeller Report on the Americas* (Chicago: Quadrangle Books, 1969).

20. U.S. Congressional Research Service, Library of Congress (various authors), *Implications of President Carter's Conventional Arms Transfer Policy,* 77-223, F, VA 15, U.S., September 22, 1977, p. 41.

21. Taken from data of U.S. Department of Defense, *Congressional Presentation, Security Assistance Program FY 1979, 1978* (Washington, D.C.: DoD, 1978). Figures for fiscal year 1978 are estimated; those for 1979 are proposed.

22. Taken from data of U.S. Department of Defense, Defense Security Assistance Agency, *Foreign Military Sales and Military Assistance Facts,* December 1977, p. 32.

23. Raimo Väyrynen, *The Transfer of Arms and Military Technology as an Aspect of Global Militarization* (Paper prepared for the Womp II meeting in Poona, India, July 2–11, 1978), p. 20.

24. From data taken from *SIPRI Yearbook 1978,* p. 254. All values are in constant 1975 US$.

25. See Raul Olmedo, "Armamentismo y ciclo económico," *Nueva Política* (Mexico), no. 5-6 (April-September 1977), p. 99.

26. See Anne Hessing Cahn and Joseph J. Kruzel, "Arms Trade in the 1980's," in A. H. Cahn, J. J. Kruzel, P. M. Dawkins, and Jacques Huntzinger, *Controlling Future Arms Trade* (New York: McGraw-Hill for the Council on Foreign Relations, 1977), pp. 67–68.

27. Congressional Research Service, *Implications of Carter's Policy,* p. 67.

28. Cahn and Kruzel, "Arms Trade in the 1980's," p. 64.

29. R. Väyrynen, "Las corporaciones trasnacionales y la transferencia de armas," in CIDE, *La dependencia militar latinoamericana* (Mexico City: CIDE, 1978), p. 27.

30. Cahn and Kruzel, "Arms Trade in the 1980's," p. 69.

31. SIPRI, *Arms Trade with the Third World,* p. 129.

32. Cahn and Kruzel, "Arms Trade in the 1980's," p. 69.

33. Steven Lydenberg, *The U.S. Corporate Role in International Arms Transfers, Weapons for the World Update Report* (New York: Council on Economic Priorities, 1977).

34. Cahn and Kruzel, "Arms Trade in the 1980's," p. 68.

35. Einaudi et al., "Transferencia de armas," p. 368.

36. SIPRI, *Arms Trade with the Third World*, p. 123.

37. Einaudi et al., "Transferencia de armas," p. 368.

38. Robin Luckham, "Militarism: Arms and the Internationalization of Capital," *IDS Bulletin* 8, no. 3 (March 1977), p. 47.

39. SIPRI, *Arms Trade with the Third World*, p. 129.

40. Väyrynen, "Las corporaciones," p. 342.

41. SIPRI, *Arms Trade with the Third World*, p. 130. Three main nationalized French companies have merged. Sud-Aviation, Nord Aviation, and SEREB became today's Aerospatiale in order to confront the major problem of limited domestic resources. In order to diminish costs Hawker Siddeley, Scottish Aviation, and British Aircraft Corporation merged into British Aerospace Corporation. British Shipbuilders was formed out of Vickers, Vosper Thornycroft, and Yarrow. Väyrynen, *Transfer of Arms*, p. 21.

42. Einaudi et al., "Transferencia de armas," in CIDE, *La dependencia*, p. 364.

43. Bob Levin and Larry Rohter, "Brazil: A Call to Arms," *Newsweek*, February 26, 1979, p. 23.

44. Ulrich Albrecht, "Arms Trade with the Third World and Domestic Arms Production," *Instant Research on Peace and Violence*, no. 1-2 (1976), p. 57.

45. Cited in Levin and Rohter, "Brazil," p. 23.

46. Lydenberg, *The U.S. Corporate Role*, p. 22.

47. Levin and Rohter, "Brazil."

48. Lydenberg, *The U.S. Coporate Role*, p. 47.

49. Einaudi et al., "Transferencia de armas," p. 364.

50. *SIPRI Yearbook 1978*, p. 229.

51. Einaudi et al., "Transferencia de armas," p. 363.

52. Väyrynen, "Transfer of Arms," p. 11.

53. Ibid., p. 15.

54. Cahn and Kruzel, "Arms Trade in the 1980's," p. 42.

55. Michael Klare, *War Without End* (New York: Vintage Books, 1972).

56. Zeb B. Bradford and Frederick J. Brown, "Apoyo del ejército a la coalición de seguridad," *Military Review*, May 1972

57. *Estrategia* (Buenos Aires), no. 24 (1973).

58. For this topic see José Medina Echeverría, "América Latina en los escenarios posibles de la distensión," *Revista de la CEPAL*, 1976, pp. 9–87; and Aníbal Pinto, "Guerra fría y distensión en América Latina," *Estudios Internacionales* (Santiago), April-June 1981.

59. Jean-Claude Buhrer, "De multiples conflicts troublent les relations entre nations latino-americaines," *Le Monde*, February 21, 1979, p. 5.

60. A further look at intraregional conflicts of interest can be found in "Pacto amazónico: Dominación o integración," *Nueva Sociedad* (Caracas), no. 37 (July-August 1979).

61. Alexander S. C. Barros, "The Diplomacy of National Security: South American International Relations in a Defrosting World," in Roland G. Hellman and H. Jon Rosenbaum, eds., *Latin America: The Search for a New International Role* (New York: Sage Publications, 1975), pp. 131–150.

62. See Jacques Huntzinger, "Regional Recipients Restraints," in Cahn et al., *Controlling Future Arms Trade*, p. 187.

5. The Transfer of Military Technology from Developed Countries

One of the factors that is frequently blamed and indeed partly responsible for the arms race in Latin America is the transfer of military technology from the arms industries of the North to the military establishments of the South. The transfer of a degree of research and development (R&D) has combined with preexisting productive capacity to sustain the development of war technology and arms production throughout Latin America.

Research and development has itself become a profitable industry, encouraging both investment and competition. Firms specializing in R&D vie not only for technological innovation but also for markets. They often pursue both by transferring military technology and production to the Third World. As the arms industry in the developed world has become saturated, production of certain weapons has been transferred through subcontracting, licensing, and coproduction agreements. Before these arrangements can work, however, the arms industry in the Third World must be sufficiently developed. The inevitable result of increased R&D activity in industrialized countries is the expansion of the arms-producing capacity of the Third World, whose arms industries are already beginning to compete with their own partners on the world market.

R&D AND THE EXPORT OF ARMS

One of the interesting features of R&D in the arms field in developed countries has been its rapid transformation into a powerful and profitable national industry.[1] The success of R&D in developed countries has stimulated the transfer of increasingly sophisticated weapons to peripheral countries; in turn generating demand in recipient countries for more weapons of even greater sophistication. Arms imports are almost invariably followed by the development of a local arms industry. Initial subcontracts and licenses become the seeds of a full-blown local arms

61

TABLE 4
Distribution of Military R&D Among Western Powers, 1960-1979

	1960-1964 Millions US$	%	1965-1969 Millions US$	%	1979 Millions US$	%
United States	7,608	84.3	7,475	82.3	14,310	70.8
United Kingdom	761	8.3	609	6.9	2,470	12.2
France	321	3.6	546	6.0	2,170	10.7
West Germany	123	1.4	206	2.3	1,015	5.0
Sweden	67	0.8	81	0.9	235	1.2
Ten other countries[a]	129	1.7	175	1.8	--	--
Total	9,017	100.0	9,088	100.0	20,200	100.0

[a]Not specified in source.

Sources: For 1960-1969: R. Väyrynen, "Military R&D as an Aspect of the Arms Race," Current Research on Peace and Violence, no. 3-4 (1978); for 1979: R. Väyrynen, "Military Research and Development and Scientific Policy," International Social Science Journal, no. 1 (1983).

industry. This process occurs most readily in developing countries that have already established a minimum industrial base. In some cases, there is already a crude arms industry that is not yet profitable enough to be included in national development programs. Licenses, subcontracts, and coproduction agreements allow these local industries to attain the same levels of profitability and expansion as the developed countries' arms industries.

On strict business criteria, the production of weapons has become a highly profitable economic activity, producing increasing returns. It is based on an established foundation of the basic sciences, which are translated into technology. Combined scientific and technological research has enabled industrialized countries to manufacture weapons that incorporate the very latest developments in the field.

The first military transfers from industrialized countries to the Third World were always in the form of finished products.[2] R&D firms kept a monopoly on the technology needed to produce weapons. In this way, they created captive markets for their products and associated spare parts. They also discouraged Third World countries from pursuing their own military R&D.

The R&D industry in the developed countries became fiercely competitive. Third World countries could not match the funds that central governments in developed countries could allocate to their arms industries (see Table 4). To give an example, the United States and France allocate funds for military electronics equivalent to 24.5 percent and 29.5 percent respectively of the total electronics markets of their economies.[3]

As long as the United States, France, and the United Kingdom dominated their respective spheres of influence in the post–World War II period, it was not necessary to resort to the sale of arms to balance trade deficits. Their overall trading situation was sufficiently strong for them to disregard any competition. However, in the 1960s the civil industries of the Federal Republic of Germany and Japan (countries that had emerged from the war without their own arms industries) began to challenge the commercial hegemony of the victors of World War II. One after another, different branches of the civil market were cornered by Japanese and German firms: shipbuilding, industrial equipment, chemicals, electronic equipment, and motors. Products from West Germany and Japan began to encroach successfully even on the domestic markets of the victorious powers. The growing competitiveness and technological efficiency of these countries considerably damaged their competitors' hitherto almost unlimited capacity to dispose of their products on the foreign market and also to control their own local markets.

As competition among industrialized nations increases, there is a tendency to view the military sector as an unexplored alternative where advantages might be exploited to balance trade between the industrialized nations themselves and between them and the Third World. This, for example, accounts for recent U.S. pressure on Japan (apart from purely military and strategic reasons) to increase its defense budget and its arms purchases.

Similarly, France is attempting to offset its trade deficit with Japan by exporting military equipment and nuclear technology.[4] The situation is similar in West Germany, which has been developing its own arms-producing capacity. As the exporting strength of this country's economy has declined, the idea of stepping up arms sales to the Third World, and especially to Arab countries, has become popular. Transfers of military material to underdeveloped countries have increased in recent years.[5]

In short, for those countries with comparative advantages in this field, arms production and exports have come to represent an effective way of competing in world markets. This was possible due to the systematic strengthening of R&D capacities. However, the transformation of R&D into a more profitable industry demanded markets larger than the mere export of arms could offer. For this reason, the growth of R&D became instrumental in changing the pattern of transfers of military technology to the Third World.

R&D has become a highly profitable industry and has in turn stimulated dynamic arms production. The nature of the transfer of military technology from developed countries to the Third World has changed considerably. From World War II through the 1960s the transfer of military technology to the Third World was mainly in the form of finished arms or weapons systems. This has only recently been superceded

TABLE 5
U.S. and Soviet Civil and Military Technology Transfer, 1963-1976

Year	U.S. SITC7[a] in millions US$ (1)	U.S. Arms Transfers (2)	Ratio: (2) as a percentage of (1)	USSR SITC7[a] in millions US$ (3)	USSR Arms Transfers (4)	Ratio: (4) as a percentage of (3)
1963	8.178	1.198	14.6	1.474	1.219	83
1967	12.573	2.230	17.7	2.088	1.920	92
1972	21.532	4.100	19.0	3.619	2.840	78
1976	49.510	5.206	10.5	6.257	3.747	60

[a]SITC7 = Civilian capital goods

Source: Peter Lock, "New International Economic Order and Armaments,"
Vierteljahresberichte, no. 77 (1979).

by transfers through subcontracting, licensing, and coproduction agreements. This change in the structure of transfers is obvious in the diminishing proportion of finished military products transferred to the Third World (Table 5).

Although there is a greater increase in the transfer of civil technology than military products, this is due in part to a drop in the rate of exports of finished weapons during the 1970s. The United States, which had doubled its arms exports in the 1960s, increased this trade by only about 25 percent between 1972 and 1976. The Soviet Union maintained a more traditional policy, transferring a steady proportion of weapons and substantially increasing exports of products for civil use. However, in recent years, because of competition with the Western industrial powers, the Soviet Union has also been obliged to transfer part of its production capacity to the Third World. Licenses to produce the MiG-21 in North Korea and in India indicate this change.

Manufacture under license is one of the most important forms of transfer of military technology to the Third World. This process enables R&D and arms industries to prolong the usefulness and profitability of military technology that may already be obsolete in supplier countries but is still competitive in the Third World. The U.S. Northrop fighter F-5E/Tiger II, the Mirage 5, the French ERC-905 armored car, and the Swedish Saab Supporter aircraft are all good examples.[6] These weapons are outdated from the point of view of U.S., French, and Swedish defense. Transferring their production to a country of the periphery and adapting to a production scale compatible with a smaller market prolong their profitability. It is disadvantageous to produce these weapons with all the corresponding infrastructure in the United States, France, or Sweden. If South Korea or Taiwan produce such arms not only for their own requirements but also for a regional or subregional area, production can be adapted to the type and level of output required by the new market.

Since the sale of technology to Third World countries includes the sale of patents, it is possible to continue to extract revenue from technologies already "exhausted" in the industrialized countries.[7] It must be stressed that the most advanced technology is never sold; only its products are. On the other hand, relatively outdated technology is readily transferred to Third World countries (Tables 6 and 7). The process of manufacture under license has enabled Third World countries to establish military industries that meet not only their own needs but also those of other Third World countries. For example, the production of arms under license in Brazil, Israel, and South Africa has enabled those countries to export a large proportion of what they produce to other Third World countries (Table 8).

Brazil has used its local arms industry to offset the huge trade deficits that resulted from the increased cost of essential oil imports.[8] Israel and South Africa enter Third World markets through the direct sale of arms to developing countries[9] and through association with other local Third World producers. This became easier recently when the United States lifted its ban on Israeli export of military products manufactured under U.S. licenses.[10] The ineffectiveness of the world embargo against South Africa has also boosted sales.

Arms production under license has permitted the export of military technology while avoiding restrictions imposed on the straight transfer of finished products. The arms industries of developed countries have become more competitive in Third World markets without having to transfer the actual technological knowledge to produce the weapons. This helps to limit the competition from new Third World arms industries.

Despite this temporary solution to the commerical problem facing R&D firms, there is still pressure to obtain increasing returns on investments, and subcontracting is one answer. This new procedure owes its origin to two sets of factors. First, R&D firms are requiring increasing investment to maintain their productivity and their competitiveness worldwide. Costs rise as the marginal productivity of these investments falls. Accordingly, new ways are sought to produce highly sophisticated weapons in regions that can offer such advantages as ample natural resources and low labor costs. These factors enable R&D firms to cut costs through subcontracting agreements. Transnational capital is pursuing the same strategy, geographically distributing different phases of production in areas where costs are lowest.

Inasmuch as R&D firms are controlled by transnational capital, depend on it, and nourish it, subcontracting has been reinforced. Through subcontracting agreements, a specific type of very specialized but partial technology is transferred. Components of sophisticated weapons—but never the complete product itself—may be manufactured. This practice has been widely adopted, as can be seen from the data on U.S. subcontracting presented in Table 9.

TABLE 6
Production of Aircraft Under Licence in the Third World, 1980

Country	Counterinsurgency Weapons	Fighters	Helicopters	Light Planes	Trainers	Transport
Argentina			Cicare CK-1	Piper Arrow-3		
Brazil	EMB-326 Xavante	MB-340[a]	AS-350M Esquilo	EML-810		
Egypt		Mirage-2000[b]	Lynx		Alpha Jet[b]	
India		Jaguar MiG-21 Bis	SA-315B Cheetah SA-316B Cheetah		Gnat T-2 Ajeet	
Indonesia			SA-330 Puma BO-105			C-212 A Avidar
North Korea		MiG-21 MF				
South Korea		F-GE Tiger-2				
Mexico	EMB-326 Xavante[b]					
Nigeria		BO-105			Arava[b]	EMB-110[b]
Pakistan		Alouette-3			Supporter Cessna-172	
Philippines			C-4M Kudu			
Taiwan		F-GE/F Tiger 2				BN-2A Islander

[a] Joint enterprise with Aermacchi Aeritalia.
[b] Planned.

Source: SIPRI, SIPRI Yearbook 1980 (London: Taylor and Francis, 1980).

TABLE 7
Production of Armored Vehicles, Missiles, and Warships Under Licence in the Third World, 1980

	Vehicles			Missiles			Warships		
Country	AC/APC/MICV[a]	LT	MBT	AAM	ATM	SAM	1. Destroyer 2. Frigate	FPB	Submarines
Argentina	VCI	AMX-13	TAM						
Brazil					Cobra 2000		1. Meco-360		Class 1700
India			Vijayanta-2 (vickers 30 ton)	AAA-2 Atoll R-550 Magic	55-II		2. Niteroi-class		Type-209
Egypt					Swingfire				
Pakistan			New						
Taiwan				AIH9J		MIM-23 Hawk			

[a]Acronyms: AC--armored car; APC--armored personnel carrier; MICV--mechanized infantry combat vehicle; LT--light tank; MBT--main battle tank; AAM--air-to-air missile; and FPB--fast patrol boat.

Source: SIPRI, SIPRI Yearbook 1980 (London: Taylor and Francis, 1980).

TABLE 8
Arms Exports from Selected Arms-Producing Countries 1970-1979
(Millions US$ at 1975 rates)

Country	Exports
Argentina	39
Brazil	349
Egypt	25
India	18
Indonesia	16
Israel	447
South Africa	150

Source: SIPRI, SIPRI Yearbook 1980 (London: Taylor and
Francis, 1980), p. 86.

TABLE 9
Foreign Operations of U.S. Producers of Military Electronics, 1974

Producer and Rank in Department of Defense Contracts	Number of Employees in Foreign Factories	Location of Operations
General Electric (1)	1,000	Singapore
RCA Corporation (22)	3,000	Singapore, Malaysia, Taiwan
Teledyne (25)	3,300	Singapore, Hong Kong, Malaysia
Fairchild (36)	13,300	Hong Kong, South Korea, Singapore, Mexico, Indonesia
Texas Instruments (14)	11,300	Singapore, Malaysia, El Salvador, Taiwan
Motorola (63)	7,800	South Korea, Mexico, Malaysia, Hong Kong
Hewlett Packard (97)	2,600	Singapore, Malaysia
Eight other firms	21,250	Singapore, Malaysia, Thailand, Indonesia, Hong Kong, Mauritius, South Korea, Mexico
Total	63,550	

Source: Helena Tuomi and Raimo Väyrynen, Transnational Corporations, Armaments and
Development (Tampere, Finland: Tampere Peace Research Institute, 1980), p. 141.

R&D AND COPRODUCTION AGREEMENTS

Coproduction agreements are the most advanced form of transferring
military technology from developed countries to the Third World. Such
agreements are generally concluded between industries with relatively
complementary levels of scientific and technological development. The

input from the industrialized countries is harnessed to locally developed military technology. In this way, Third World arms industries receive an added stimulus for their own expansion. This phenomenon is due to the dynamic quality of R&D in developed countries and in those Third World countries that either have their own R&D industry or have been particularly favored by arms manufacturers in developed countries.

As R&D requires more and more investment in order to remain competitive and win markets, the pressure for sizable returns increases. Merely selling weapons is not enough to attain the necessary profit levels at a time when the importers' economic capacities are decreasing, even though their financial resources are increasing. Coproduction agreements help to solve the problem of overequipping Third World armed forces by establishing a dependent export industry.

Argentina is one of the countries of the Third World with a long history of military R&D.[11] Its first attempt to produce military equipment was in 1920. In 1941 the Direccion General de Fabricaciones Militares (DGFM) strengthened state activity in this area by linking it to the general industrialization effort. Because of Argentina's neutrality during World War II, the United States excluded it from all wartime liaison—necessitating the independent development of its arms industry. From 1945 on the DGFM involved all branches of the armed forces in the manufacture of arms. The air force, with the help of German technicians, began to design and manufacture aircraft, including fighter-bombers and transport planes. The navy designed and built boats in 1938 at the Rio Santiago shipyards, and later produced patrol launches and frigates. The army manufactured heavy artillery, machine guns, and various types of munitions with German assistance. In 1940 the Rosario factory began to develop and manufacture a series of machine guns that are still in use.

This initial impetus from German cooperation helped to establish Argentine R&D, which though relatively modest (no more than 1 percent of GNP has ever been allocated to R&D), has provided continuous support for the arms industry. In 1958 the National Council of Scientific and Technological Research became the main agent for this type of research. Likewise, the National Institute of Industrial Technology, the National Atomic Energy Commission and the National Commission for Space Research have also enabled Argentina to develop a military and nuclear industry that, with the aid of licenses and foreign technical assistance, is the most powerful in Latin America. These R&D activities have also been linked to the development of the state steel and aluminum industry and the vehicle industries. The Direccion General de Fabricaciones Militares (General Directorate for Ordnance Production) and the Direccion Nacional de la Industria e Investigaciones Aeronauticas (National Directorate of Aeronautical Industries and Research) design and produce aerospace equipment under the supervision of the air force. In the 1950s they manufactured combat aircraft such as the IA-60 Pucará fighter and the Cicare CH-11 Cobri helicopter; in the 1960s they concentrated on the manufacture of transport and counterinsurgency aircraft such as the IA-60 Guarani 11 and the IA-58 Pucará. The DGFM produced aircraft for civilian use and assembled the French AMX-13 tank. Under a coproduction contract with the West German firm of Thyseen-Henschel, Argentina is developing light and medium tanks and armored vehicles for personnel transport. The Astilleros y Fabricaciones Navales Estatales (State Shipyards and Naval Manufactures) produce locally designed naval equipment such as frigates and missile patrol boats. They also assemble submarines with West German components. By an agreement with the Dornier firm, Argentina is now undertaking the construction of a jet trainer with limited capacity for tactical support missions. This aircraft, the IA-63, will be manufactured by the National Directorate of Aeronautical Industries and Research in the province of Cordoba and was scheduled to go into series production in 1985.[12]

Coproduction has become one of the most effective stimuli of the Argentine arms industry. Supported by their own R&D base, the Argentine arms industries are in a position to increase their technological capacity. It would therefore be no surprise if their current aircraft and tank coproduction agreements are followed by agreements for the construction of boats with Spain, submarines with West Germany, and coastal patrol boats with France.

The Brazilian aeronautics industry is another example of the effect of strong indigenous R&D on local arms production.[13] The Empresa Brasileira de Aeronautica (Brazilian Aeronautics Company, or EMBRAER), which began operations in January 1970, is the culmination of an effort to develop Brazil's own technology in the field of civil and military aviation. EMBRAER covers the needs of the Brazilian air force in the following areas: (1) basic training planes with ground attack capability; (2) pressurized and nonpressurized twin-engine turboprop planes for transporting personnel and equipment; (3) marine patrol, search and rescue aircraft; and (4) special models for photogrammetry and calibration. With its capacity, industrial plant, and own R&D, EMBRAER has become a major subcontractor and coproducer. It manufactures the fuselage of the Northrop F-5E, and is coproducing AMX fighter aircraft with the Italian firm Aermachi.[14]

Mexico is also seeking to join the trend of coproduction in order to strengthen its R&D capacities. Mexico currently manufactures armored vehicles, and is attempting to produce assault rifles for its army.[15] The Mexican government is encouraging national development of science and technology, which will certainly contribute to the country's nascent arms industry. Funds are being allocated for R&D projects in the chemical industry, telecommunications, transportation, metallurgy, electronics, engineering, and automobile industries. The Ministry of National Defense has been very active in obtaining funds for such activities. In fact, all twenty-five projects submitted by the ministries of defense and the navy were approved.[16] It is quite possible that the Mexican defense industry will coproduce the Argentine TAM tank in the near future.

The foregoing shows the importance of R&D in establishing local arms industries in Latin America. Argentina, with its own scientific and technological development plus the initial assistance from German advisers, shows the importance of R&D as a first step in the development of an arms industry. Likewise, Brazil's aeronautics industry indicates that local initiative in R&D makes it possible to attain higher levels of military industrialization, which later allows coproduction of much more sophisticated weaponry than could be obtained by entirely national production. The final example of Mexico, a country with no defense industry, illustrates that in order to develop an armored-vehicle industry efforts must first be made to establish an R&D process in which the national defense authorities are interested.

Research and development growth in the countries of the Third World is also being transferred to other developing countries with less technological capacity. Examples are the possible Argentine-Venezuelan agreement to coproduce the Pucará aircraft, and the plans to reequip the Chinese armored M-41s by ENGESA, the Brazilian armored-vehicle industry.[17] Through such activities the arms-producing countries of the Third World are beginning to compete with the industrialized countries. Brazil competes with West Germany in the production of armored vehicles; the Israeli Lavi competes with U.S. FX aircraft.

Financial factors also contribute to the transfer of military technology. International overliquidity caused by the breakup of the Bretton Woods system and high OPEC oil prices has allowed the accumulation in the hands of transnational financial interests of large amounts of foreign currency. It is difficult to find an outlet for this money in industrial projects or traditional economic activities in developed countries. One way of utilizing this abundant liquidity has been to offer short- and medium-term credit to Third World countries. For the first time these countries have had access to very flexible funds. This new credit, in addition to being readily accessible, has been increasingly freed of the constraints and controls previously imposed by the developed countries' foreign-aid policies. The Third World countries have therefore had much more freedom to implement their own policies—including the acquisition of military technology.

This tendency was reinforced by high oil prices and resulting deficits in the balance of payments. The industrialized powers, seeking to compensate for their growing deficits, began to encourage weapons sales to those countries that had gained excessive liquidity. The tremendous funds in the hands of the petroleum-producing countries was recycled, in part, through the transfer of military technology. Iran is one example.

For the majority of the Third World countries, especially those without oil, the possibility of obtaining financial resources on the international capital market is accompanied, however, by a countervailing increase

TABLE 10
Indicators of Economic Growth and Militarization in Latin America, 1973-1980
(In millions US$)

Year	Gross National Product[a]	Military Expenditure[a]	Arms Imports[a]	External Debt
1973	465,000	6,800	869	42,800
1974	497,000	8,800	638	
1975	512,000	9,800	757	
1976	535,000	8,600	1,176	
1977	558,000	9,400	1,220	104,200
1978	580,000	9,400	1,601	
1979	612,000	8,700	1,610	
1980	644,000	9,400	1,612	205,400
Average yearly rate of increase	4.78	5.49	11.86	25.11

[a]Constant 1979 US$

Sources: For GNP, Military Expenditures, and Arms Imports: U.S. Arms Control and Disarmament Agency, World Military Expenditures and Arms Transfers 1971-1980 (Washington, D.C.: ACDA, 1983); for External Debt: Interamerican Development Bank, Progreso económico y social en América Latina (Washington, D.C.: 1982), p. 182.

in their foreign debt and deficits. This is the case throughout Latin America (see Table 10). Countries with a basic industrial infrastructure have therefore attempted to shift from imports to production of weapons. The local arms industry becomes a partial supplier for the armed forces, contributing to a positive balance of payments through import substitution and, in some cases, through exports to other Third World countries.

EFFECTS OF THE TRANSFER OF MILITARY TECHNOLOGY

The transfer of military technology to the Third World has had both sociopolitical and economic effects. On the sociopolitical level, the armed forces in Latin America have become increasingly isolated as they develop a level of professional expertise that has little to do with local society. They become increasingly linked with the world of transnational corporations and industrialized countries. The transfer of military technology thus contributes to the development of a social sector endowed with relative autonomy vis-à-vis the rest of society, and to the introduction of foreign life-styles and technology that are irrelevant to the problems of the majority. It alienates social sectors that might otherwise contribute to local development. It also further distorts the distribution of income and educational opportunities in favor of sectors that mediate between Third World countries and suppliers of technology.

A second factor closely linked to the first concerns the integration of armed forces into an international system of military relations. This system is composed of a local military complex whose technological development keeps it independent of the national environment, together with a transnational industrial and military complex.

Leading military groups come to see their expansion as a social sector, their prestige, and their ability to maintain their life-style and employment as contingent upon the link with the transnational military-industrial complex. They develop a specific, corporatist view of national needs. They acquire a particular notion of the type of development and type of state that will be compatible with maintaining their transnational ties and that will guarantee their flow of resources. Being fundamentally dependent upon transnational groups, these strongly corporatist military elites share their ideological concerns and alienate themselves equally from the popular and civilian parts of their own societies. Military forces even become internal political and social "representatives" of multi-national arms-producing interests.

Local armed forces advocate development models that guarantee resources for massive imports of military technology. The involvement of military elites in the international transfer of military technology distorts national defense policies and encourages standardization, regardless of differences in national needs and political objectives. Specific military technology is designed with a particular conception of national defense and with specific political and strategic objectives in mind, and when Third World countries import military technology created for and suited to the needs of arms-producing powers, they are importing the answer to a question they have not asked. The transfer of military technology therefore implies the creation of needs for which that particular technology is appropriate. Third World armed forces thus adopt the framework of national defense ideologies and strategies for which the purchased arms and technology are useful.

In the industrialized countries political and military policy determine military technological structure; in Third World countries it is the structure that determines the policy. In this way, national defense policies consistent with the real needs of the people are supplanted. This has international implications, for it affects the way governments view the prevailing international situation. The logic behind military buildup and constant preparation for war in the exporting countries is thus reproduced on a local scale.

Another important effect of the transfer of military technology to Third World countries is the increased use of force in local conflicts. The possession of sophisticated military technology and advanced production capability enables Third World political leaders to escalate conflict to greater levels than before. At the same time, this high level of technology does not allow the total overall mobilization of national resources that would be consistent with the military program. The military effort remains relatively limited and excludes a large number of domestic protagonists who can do little more than witness the conflict. Finally, the ready availability of military technology facilitates and stimulates regional and subregional arms competition, creating among governments the illusion that they can in this way increase their power and influence over potentially hostile neighbors.

The transfer of sophisticated military technology thus alters both the quantity and the quality of conflicts and of the relations between Third World countries. The availability of arms facilitates the involvement of the great powers in conflicts in which they would normally have no direct interest. Because the large arms-supplying countries regard military technology as a weapon of political influence and a factor of national prestige, they cannot be indifferent to the outcome of conflicts between countries of the Third World. The supplier/purchaser relationship and the dependence of one military system upon another results in these systems being viewed as a political investment that must be safeguarded. The outcome of conflicts thus becomes part of the logic of East-West confrontations as the great powers seek to maintain their spheres of influence. The transfer of military technology produced by industrialized countries thus tends to export those countries' conflicts and to transform the Third World countries into a battlefield—in a very literal sense— of the conflict in which the great powers cannot engage directly because of the danger of nuclear exchange.

The converse is also true. Trafficking in arms transforms the great-power suppliers of military technology into hostages of local conflicts whose origins may have no direct bearing on the problems of the developed countries. Upon becoming suppliers to peripheral countries, the central countries find themselves obliged to support politico-military regimes and enterprises whose goals and policies may seriously compromise their own values. These involvements, spurred by the fear of being supplanted by competitors for direct military influence, jeopardize the general climate of détente between the blocs. The role this type of confrontation and the consequent local arms escalation have played in creating a climate unfavorable to disarmament and détente should be underscored.

The economic effects of the transfer of military technology are also considerable. Although some countries that undertake the production of weapons see their balance of payments favorably affected, there are serious distortions as well. In the first place, an internal technological imbalance occurs that widens the gap between the modern high-productivity sector and the large underdeveloped economic hinterland, which is neither drawn along nor stimulated by arms-related activities.

The technology introduced by weapons production is generally quite sophisticated and involves complex components. The local economic base is not greatly affected by defense spending, which makes few demands on the local economy for inputs and provides no major spin-

TABLE 11
Per Capita Public Spending on Defense, Education and Health in Latin America, 1980
(In thousand US$)

	Defense (1)	Education (2)	Health (3)	(2):(1)	(3):(1)
Argentina	58	157	22	2.70	0.37
Bolivia	19	38	11	2.00	0.57
Brazil	13	63	32	4.84	2.46
Chile	132	113	58	0.85	0.43
Colombia	12	24	16	2.00	1.33
Costa Rica	--	117	25	--	--
Cuba	114	162	50	1.42	0.43
Dominican Republic	19	24	22	1.26	1.15
Ecuador	26	49	16	1.88	0.61
El Salvador	11	29	12	2.63	1.09
Guatemala	14	21	16	1.50	1.14
Honduras	12	20	11	1.66	0.91
Jamaica	9	76	27	8.44	3.00
Mexico	11	78	11	7.09	1.00
Nicaragua	28	26	37	0.92	1.32
Panama	9	87	84	9.66	9.33
Paraguay	21	18	5	0.85	0.23
Peru	26	19	9	0.73	0.34
Uruguay	90	78	37	0.86	0.41
Venezuela	46	188	97	4.08	2.10

Source: Ruth Leger Sivard, World Military and Social Expenditures 1983, copyright
World Priorities, Washington, D.C. 20007, U.S.A. Used by permission.

offs. Labor is very specialized; manufactured inputs are only partially produced locally or are directly imported; raw materials are similarly imported. The only local input is cheap unskilled labor. Secondly, the products imported or produced locally by the defense sector do not contribute to the total supply of goods and services for the nonmilitary economy as a whole. The military sector thus diverts substantial capital, removing it from the productive circuits of the economy.

The growth of military technology hence takes place independent of technological development in the areas of civilian production and is unrelated to the average technical level of a peripheral country. A good example is Argentina, which has a growing capacity in military technology, including nuclear technology, but whose civilian industries are experiencing a dangerous decline in productivity owing to a lack of technical innovation and the anti-industrial policies of the government.

A further cost is the social development foregone in favor of military production. Military industry absorbs scarce resources in the Third

World—resources that might otherwise have been used to improve the social infrastructure and raise the living standard of the population. Funds for long-term social investment badly needed in Third World countries are diverted instead to the international arms race (see Table 11).

NOTES

This chapter is a revised version of Augusto Varas and Fernando Bustamante, "The Effects of R&D and the Transfer of Military Technology to the Third World," *International Social Science Journal*, no. 1 (1983).

1. The topic here is the profitability of the arms industry rather than military expenditure per se, although the two are obviously related. As its production exceeds domestic consumption, the arms industry is becoming an increasingly substantial source of profits. In some cases, military spending seems to have positive effects, contradicting forecasts of blocked development: "On the other hand, technological 'spin-off' from military expenditure may have the opposite effect, stimulating growth: for example, higher productivity growth through R&D in military industries may increase growth rates for these countries." Dan Smith and Ron Smith, "Military Expenditure, Resources and Development," April 1980 (mimeo).

2. For a current view of this aspect of North-South economic relations and their prospects for the 1980s see Bernard Lietaer, *L'Amérique latine et l'Europe demain: Le role des multinationales européennes dans les années 1980* (Paris, Presses Universitaires de France, 1980).

3. See Helena Tuomi and Raimo Väyrynen, *Transnational Corporations, Armaments and Development* (Tampere, Finland: Tampere Peace Research Institute, 1980), pp. 56–57.

4. *Le Monde*, April 22, 1981.

5. *Strategic Week*, January 12–18, 1981. For sales by West Germany, especially ships and submarines, see SIPRI, *SIPRI Yearbook 1980* (London: Taylor & Francis, 1980), p. 79.

6. Ibid., pp. 41–43.

7. Cf. Raimo Väyrynen, "International Patent System, Technological Dominance and Transnational Corporations," in Kirsten Worm, ed., *Industrialization, Development and the Demands for a New International Economic Order* (Copenhagen: Samfundsvidenskabeligt Forlag, 1978).

8. According to unofficial sources, Brazil sold between US$700 and 800 million worth of military equipment in 1980, US$1 billion worth in 1981, and US$2 billion in 1982.

9. Ignacio F. Klich, "L'Amérique Latine, principal client de l'industrie d'armement israelienne," *Le Monde Diplomatique*, September 1980.

10. See *Strategic Week*, November 24–30, 1980, and *Herald Wire Service*, November 1, 1980.

11. The following analysis is a summary of an article by Edward S. Milenki, "Arms Production and National Security in Argentina," *Journal of Interamerican Studies*, August 1980.

12. *Defensa*, no. 21 (January 1980).

13. For our data on Brazil we referred to "EMBRAER: Alas del Brasil," in ibid., and Clovis Brigagao, "The Case of Brazil: Fortress or Paper Curtain?" *Impact* 31, no. 1 (January-March 1981), p. 17.

14. *Strategic Latin American Affairs*, April 3, 1980.

15. *Strategic Latin American Affairs*, January 1980.

16. National Council of Science and Technology, *Mexico's Programme for Science and Technology, 1978–1982* (Mexico City, n.d.).

17. *Strategic Latin American Affairs*, March 13 and May 22, 1980.

6. Perceptions of Security and Conflict and the Arms Race

Attempts to explain the arms race in Latin America have utilized diverse analytical models. Most recognize that the accumulative interaction among states tends to escalate their arms purchases. The various models have offered valuable heuristic insights into the phenomenon, yet as the Latin American reality has become increasingly complex in recent years, these schemes of analysis no longer apply. With the increasing scope, diversity, and intricacy of political relations among all countries of the world, the dynamics of the arms trade in Latin America can no longer be explained by the simple actions and reactions of neighboring countries. Consequently, we must expand our conception of the problem to include the global context.

The dynamics of the Latin American arms race is affected by diverse internal and external factors. This chapter seeks to establish the logical and analytical connections between the internal, national, and international levels of the arms race to reveal its nature and causes. My purpose is to arrive at a conceptual formulation that integrates the national and international dimensions of the arms trade and provides a framework or foundation for future studies on the same subject. With these goals in mind, I have departed from conventional analyses, focusing instead on the role that the perception of security plays when armed states formulate their reaction to a given event. My hypothesis, illustrated by an analysis of cases in the region, is that arms expenditures in Latin America are an adaptive, although incorrect, response to the changes in the security context of each country in the region.

PERCEPTIONS AND FALLACIES

Previous analyses of the arms race have all presumed rationality in the actions of both individuals and groups. According to this perspective, the actions of a state will be correctly and identically interpreted by all observers. Such is the supposition within the paradigm of Lewis F. Richardson, who theorized that the military expenditures of a state are related to the actions and decisions of a potentially belligerent neighboring state. The objective variables are arms expenditures, their rates of increase, and the time periods involved. Richardson feels justified in proclaiming that " 'hostility' as reflected in armaments is a quantifiable variable."[1] Any change in the rates of increase of arms expenditures will be perceived as a gesture of hostility by one state toward another, and the lagging state will react by augmenting its own rate of increase. The arms race results from this perception of hostile gestures.[2]

This same hypothesis subsequently led Anatol Rapoport to state that "the tyranny of strategic thinking [is] governed by preoccupation with individual rationality."[3] In his opinion the analogies of Herman Kahn ("game of chicken") and Thomas Shelling ("prisoner dilemma") put too great an emphasis on the rationality of each individual rather than on the rationality of the system, which could lead to common benefits. "Collective rationality can be realized if the players can reach an enforceable agreement to act in their common interest."[4] However, both the emphasis on an "individual rationality" that leads to mutual destruction and the emphasis on a "collective rationality" that could lead to mutual cooperation are based on the assumption that the decisions and actions of the players are rational or "logical."

Other authors have pointed out that this assumption is valid neither generally nor in its application to specific cases of arms competition. It implies, for example, an accurate interpretation of situations by those making decisions. James Burton states:

> It is at the point of perception that decision-making commences, and any misperceptions automatically render responses inappropriate. If power were perceived as the motivation of other states, certain defensive policies would follow logically; if participation were perceived as the drive of international society, policies would take different forms.[5]

The assumption of rationality on the part of actor and opponent, and within their relations, is flawed and obscures real elements of international arms dynamics.

The principal errors of the rationality approach have been disclosed by Robert Jervis, who locates fourteen questionable sub-assumptions within the approach. Because actors tend to formulate their views and perceptions prematurely, they often wind up seeing just what they expect to see in the actions of their opponents. The entire set of perceptions is prejudiced and rationality vanishes. Jervis further asserts that "there is an overall tendency for decision-makers to see other states as more hostile than they are"[6]—and not only more hostile, but also more unified, integrated, and single-minded.

Jervis pursues his critique by considering the distortion potential. Information about neighboring states is overvalued and distorted to suit expectations, as is a state's self-image. Jervis's analysis leads him to proclaim that "at the roots of many important disputes about policies lie differing perceptions." Jervis insists that threats "are more apt to work and the deterrence model is more apt to apply when: 1) the other side sees the cost of standing firm as very high . . . this will be the case when: 1a) the other side is relatively weak or vulnerable; 1b) the other places an especially high subjective value on preserving the lives and properties of its citizens."[7]

Because the rationality assumption of deterrence has such a limited application, neither Kahn's model nor the "dilemma of the prisoner" can be usefully applied to interstate rivalry, as both paradigms presume that potential opponents are rational; that they have equivalent or superior military power or realize that any aggressive conduct will escalate into open conflict.

Neither the simple model of reciprocal perceptions of threat nor the assumption of rationality apply to Latin America. A. L. George identifies eight conditions that should exist in order for a threat to elicit the desired effect. He indicates that "the initiator's perception of a defender's commitment may be a necessary condition for deterrence, but it is not a *sufficient* condition."[8] If the initiator appreciates the role of perception in the deterrence value of the defender's commitment, that deterrence potential is of course diminished even further. George therefore concludes that any "assessment," however rational it may seem, does not imply in itself the ability to deter an opponent from attacking or defending itself at a high cost.

Perceptions of deterrence are fundamental to the rational action-reaction models that have been applied to the arms race. However, George asserts that even the coercive strategy of an ultimatum requires a set of conditioning agents in order to obtain the desired effect. Thus, he argues that "only seldom—only when a special set of conditions is present—is it feasible . . . to undertake what has been called the ultimatum approach."[9] These conditions include asymmetry of power in favor of the initiator of the ultimatum; clarity of the initiator's objectives; a sense of urgency to achieve goals; adequate internal political support; a real possibility of military options; the opponent's fear of an unacceptable escalation; and a clear resolution of the conflict.

Bruce Russett poses another set of conditions,[10] noting that the levels of interdependence among possible rivals make deterrence credible when it endangers the common interests, and perhaps survival, of both. This supposes rationality on the part of both actors. Yet Russett's conditions for deterrence fail to explain the reactions to hostility expressed by increases in arms expenditures.

Perceptions of threats cannot be reduced to a simple equation of hostility as an opponent's increased arms expenditure. Rather, perceptions of and reactions to threats exist within a highly fluid environment in which agents, or states, are continually redefining their positions. Deterrence, or in other words the perception of hostility, is determined by changes in the security context of each agent. As Raymond Boudon states, "The interdependent system is characterized by the fact that the actions of the agents within the system engender collective phenomena which are outside of the will or intentions of the particular agents."[11]

The downfall of an interdependent system may be produced either by system factors[12] or by a combination of internal and external factors.[13] Each actor may be characterized as "initiator" or "recipient." As a general hypothesis, we can assert that the destruction of an interdependent system of regional security, be it induced by global changes or by internal modifications, will be accompanied by an increase in arms expenditures. Changes in national and international variables, which constitute one dimension of interdependent relations, encourage states to increase their weapons and overall military power.

Security systems imply international ties, which in turn imply stability in the internal situation. Any significant variations within a state will require the readjustment of both the internal and external situation. In other words, instability in internal-external relations leads to an arms buildup. This behavior is neither logical nor rational; it is merely the adaptive reaction of an agent to a changing environment.

Why is this adaptive reaction associated with an increase in military expenditures? Changes in a security situation require new evaluations, and actors who see their security arrangements shifting tend to overvalue the hostility of potential opponents. In this context, increasing military expenditures are not so much a method of intimidating an opponent (a supposedly rational but ineffective action). They are rather a way of temporarily compensating for the deficit in the security system evoked by internal or external changes. Military expenditures indicate imbalance in a security system. Meant as a deterrent, increased spending is more often interpreted as a new manifestation of hostility. Beyond the logic of the particular "actors," an arms buildup signals a deficit within a security system that is generating a feeling of insecurity.

Agents within an interdependent system feel threatened by alterations in the global security context. Their perceptions of threat do not express a simple awareness of the arms buildup of an antagonist, but spring rather from transformations and weaknesses *within* a security system. The degree to which actors feel threatened will determine the level of "adaptive" arms buildup. Models that describe a type of "contagion effect"[14] cannot elucidate the complexity of this phenomenon, nor can they explain cases in which the arms buildup of one state is not equivalent to that of its neighbor. Simple binary explanations miss the complex and irrational nature of the arms race and, as a consequence, have little predictive value. The following examination of specific Latin American cases will show instead how variations within a security context lead states to stockpile weapons.

TABLE 12
Evolution of Cuban Military Expenditures, 1965-1974 (1965=100)

1966	1967	1968	1969	1970	1971	1972	1973	1974
97.3	110.4	127.2	101.3	111.4	106.7	103.4	107.7	97.6

Source: U.S. Arms Control and Disarmament Agency, World Military Expenditures and Arms Transfers (Washington, D.C.: ACDA, 1975).

THE LATIN AMERICAN SECURITY
CONTEXT AND ITS ALTERATIONS

The Cuban case is of primary interest. Since 1959 its security context has been entirely distinct from that of other nations in the area. If we ignore the effect of the Bay of Pigs invasion, Tables 12 and 13 indicate that Cuban military expenditures peaked in 1968 and again in 1978–1979 (expenditures have dropped since 1979).

Neither the increase in 1968 nor the decrease that followed can be understood outside of the security context of Cuba, which had widened and become more complex after the Cuban Revolution. Along with the constant danger of another U.S.-backed invasion, Cuban support for Che Guevara's revolutionary strategies in Latin America and the contradictory messages that it received from the Soviet Union were also decisive in the late 1960s. Cuba's argument with the Soviets over oil deliveries at the end of 1967 followed Cuban criticism of the Soviet invasion of Czechoslovakia and Soviet disapproval over Cuba's support of Latin American revolutionaries. Cuba reacted to these changes in its relations with the Soviet Union by increasing its military expenditures, to ensure protection in the event of isolation from the Soviet Union.

In 1978–1979, despite détente with the United States during the Carter administration and the exchange of liaison officers, Cuba once again increased its expenditures far above the historical average. The action was not provoked by corresponding increases in countries potentially belligerent to Cuba; the danger of U.S. intervention was constant and it was in any case impossible for Cuba to achieve military parity with this superpower. Instead, the increase reflected Cuban involvement in Angola and Ethiopia. Cuba's commitment to African national liberation

TABLE 13
Cuban Military Expenditures: 1970-1979 (1970=100)

1971	1972	1973	1974	1975	1976	1977	1978	1979
99.1	99.7	110.3	117.7	124.1	n.a.	n.a.	275.8	282.4

Source: U.S. Arms Control and Disarmament Agency, World Military Expenditures and Arms Transfers (Washington, D.C.: ACDA, 1982).

TABLE 14
Military Expenditures in Central America: 1975-1979 (1975=100)

	1976	1977	1978	1979
El Salvador	103.2	109.6	141.9	132.2
Guatemala	108.3	136.6	98.3	93.3
Honduras	118.1	122.7	140.9	136.3
Nicaragua	105.1	107.6	107.6	100.0
Panama	94.1	94.1	100.0	82.3

Source: U.S. Arms Control and Disarmament Agency, World Military Expenditures and Arms Transfers (Washington, D.C.: ACDA, 1982).

broadened its security context. Threats to Angolan independence from South Africa and the danger of counterrevolution in Ethiopia were seen as serious threats to Cuba's role in world politics and to its revolution as well, threats equal to the danger of isolation from the Soviet Union or of invasion from the United States. Cuba had defined its security context to include countries outside the usual regional and ideological-political limits of other neighboring countries.

Central America

Another interesting case concerns the current militarism and arms race in Central America. If we exclude Costa Rica (which has no military expenditures), we find a subregional reality that cannot be explained by the simple perception of threat from a neighbor. A satisfactory analysis requires an awareness of alterations in the whole subregional situation.

In the first place, the case of Costa Rica contradicts the "contagion effect" theory. Costa Rica defines its security more in diplomatic than military terms, and consequently, the arms buildup of neighbors is not taken as a sign of hostility by Costa Rica. As we can see from Table 14, arms expenditures in the rest of Central America are sizable, and the dynamics involved are complex.

Nicaragua began its military buildup under the Somoza regime, which perceived a threat from Sandinista guerrillas and responded by purchasing equipment oriented to counterinsurgency. Yet Nicaraguan military expenditures did not reach the net levels shown by Guatemala, for example. In El Salvador, the threat to the government also originated from internal revolutionary forces, and Salvadoran military expenditures were similarly oriented to counterinsurgency warfare. Despite increases in the arms expenditures of El Salvador and Honduras (which perceives a military-ideological threat from Nicaragua), Guatemala did not increase its expenditures as tensions in that region increased. Instead, Guatemala reduced its expenditures. A similar pattern is found in Panama.

This data indicates that the perception of threat, even in a zone as homogeneous as Central America, varies radically. Military expenditures do not exhibit the patterns expected from an accumulative model. On the contrary, in each case the perception of threat and its nature are associated with the specific security context of each state. Britain's resolution of the dispute over Belize made it unnecessary for Guatemala to intensify that conflict, yet Guatemala did feel obligated to redefine its own security context, integrating the new power configuration in the region. As the Sandinista revolution was consolidated, the security context of Nicaragua became more dependent upon political alliances than upon its military capacity to deter U.S. invasion. Honduras and El Salvador both increased expenditures; Panama reduced its spending once the Canal problem was resolved. In sum, in Central America there is no "contagion effect," and models based upon simple perceptions of threat do not apply.

The Venezuelan Case

It is important to analyze the situation of Venezuela in the light of our general hypothesis, as Venezuelan levels of military expenditures and arms imports appear unrelated to internal situations or border conflicts, despite some rivalries with Colombia and Guyana. Venezuela's security context is defined particularly by its ties with the United States, and Venezuela has become not a U.S. intermediary in the region but rather a U.S. substitute in the Central American and Caribbean zones. The Carter administration's policy of avoiding direct involvement in this subregion and of moderating the patterns of direct intervention left a political-military space that Venezuela has filled. The internal political consensus in Venezuela provides broad support for pro-American, anti-Castro measures, and has stimulated Venezuela to fill the subregional vacuum, particularly by augmenting its naval power. The development of a submarine and antisubmarine attack force indicates that Venezuela's definition of security includes its ability to act in the Caribbean zone and stresses its historical aspiration to participate in NATO. The primary stimulant to Venezuelan military expenditures has been the change in its security context—and the only factor that changed between 1970 and 1979 was the U.S. position in the subregion. In this case, it was not the introduction of a newly aggressive actor into the region but rather the withdrawal of one that led Venezuela to increase its arms expenditures.

Peru, Chile, and Argentina

Turning to the cases of Peru and Chile, we again see the weaknesses of the binary active/reactive model and the importance of attending to the international context of security and its impact on subregional situations. First of all, the perception of threat between Chile and Peru has not always generated increases in military expenditures. The pressures

TABLE 15
Military Expenditures in Chile and Peru, 1965-1972 (1965=100)

	1966	1967	1968	1969	1970	1971	1972
Chile	117.6	108.8	116.0	114.4	127.2	172.0	166.4
Peru	96.6	129.0	147.4	126.3	136.8	146.3	155.3

Source: U.S. Arms Control and Disarmament Agency, World Military Expenditures and Arms Transfers (Washington, D.C.: ACDA, 1975).

brought by the Chilean army in 1969 to increase military expenditures were not related merely to Peruvian increases. Rather, the arms buildup in this subregion was a response to the Peruvian military coup of 1968. The Chilean army sought an increase not to exceed Peru's military power, but to achieve parity with Peru, whose military capability had been built up over many years. In 1973, the Peruvian military responded to the Chilean military coup similarly, increasing its weapons supplies and accepting Soviet military aid. The Peruvian increases were at smaller *rates* than the Chilean ones, but the *levels* of expenditures continued favorable to Peru because Peru was so far ahead to begin with. Peru's military expenditures reached their greatest level in 1977, when Chile's initiative to resolve the problem of Bolivia's demand for an outlet to the sea was altering the security context once again. Peru's perception of instability and mutability of interdependent security relations propelled the increase in military expenditures.

Only in 1971 (Table 15), during the Popular Unity government, did Chile surpass the growth rates of Peru's military expenditures. This cannot be explained by the perception of potential danger on the northern border. It was instead a response to an altered Chilean security context brought about by the inauguration of the Allende government, which threatened to jeopardize all U.S.-Chilean military relations. Chile's internal political situation had a sizable impact on its external military ties. Although the stated "logic" of the respective military actors may have been that of mutual danger and hostility, in practice they were addressing a perceived security deficit induced by internal alterations (Peru in 1968 and Chile in 1970) by purchasing arms.

After the Chilean military coup, the situation became more complex. Common factors in the security context of the Southern Cone acquired greater relevance and modified the definition of the security context for each of the actors. Under the Lanusse government, Argentina attempted to diversify its international ties and increase domestic political participation. The government was run by Peronist civilians. Argentine-Chilean relations were better during this period than any other time until the 1972 nonaggression pact. However, the Argentine-Chilean security context was altered by two simultaneous events: internal political instability

TABLE 16
Military Expenditures in Argentina and Chile, 1973-1979 (1970=100)

	1973	1974	1975	1976	1977	1978	1979
Argentina	87.1	106.8	146.1	148.7	166.9	182.2	174.0
Chile	138.0	255.0	180.5	79.8	105.3	131.1	129.8
Peru	128.5	131.5	177.1	207.2	302.6	224.7	170.7

Source: U.S. Arms Control and Disarmament Agency, World Military
Expenditures and Arms Transfers (Washington, D.C.: ACDA, 1982).

combined with armed opposition from the leftist People's Revolutionary
Army (Ejercito Revolucionario del Pueblo, ERP) in Argentina, and the
military coup in Chile. Consequently, in 1975, in the middle of its
internal political crisis, Argentina increased its military expenditures by
approximately 40 percent. Although Chile's military expenditures had
risen sharply in 1974 after the military coup, Britain was at that time
mediating the border dispute between Chile and Argentina. Increased
Chilean expenditures did not therefore alter the Argentine security
context. Internal armed opposition from the left did. Only later, when
Argentina rejected the British arbitration, was an action/reaction effect
produced. This explains the simultaneous increases in 1977 through 1979
(Table 16).

In this same subregional context of security—or insecurity—Peru's
reaction was neither simple nor unequivocal. Helan Jaworski noted that
although Peruvian-U.S. relations improved during the Morales Bermudez
administration, "the Armed Forces decided that the pressures and eventual
conflicts . . . recommended not the disarmament proposed in the
Declaration of Ayacucho, but, on the contrary, an accelerated arms
buildup."[15] This was a sequel to the experience of Velasco Alvarado's
administration, whose military relations were not as diversified as the
Peruvian armed forces would have liked. In 1976, Chile and Bolivia
decided to attempt a resolution to Bolivia's lack of an outlet to the sea.
This encouraged speculation about the possibility of conflict in Peru.
Both internal and external factors thus led to Peru's increased arms
expenditures in 1977. If the situation is not seen from this dual perspective,
one falls into the simple assertion that all Peruvian military expenditures
of the period reflected the fear of confrontation with Chile. Peru's
perception of its security context was altered by a Chilean initiative of
peace, not by a hostile gesture. The peaceful gesture was accompanied
by the alteration of the security context established by the treaties signed
by Chile and Peru in 1929.

Brazil

As a final case, we may look at Brazil. This country has sustained its
increases in military expenditures regardless of national and international

TABLE 17
Brazilian Arms Imports and Exports: 1974-1979 (in millions 1978 US$)

	1974	1975	1976	1977	1978	1979
Imports	78	119	158	107	210	183
Exports	0	35	90	21	100	55

Source: U.S. Arms Control and Disarmament Agency, World Military Expenditures and Arms Transfers (Washington, D.C.: ACDA, 1982).

conditions, with an important jump in 1976. During the 1970s, the Brazilian security context was strengthened pari passu with Brazil's economic development and growing international political importance. The increases may be explained by the relationship between arms imports and exports in Brazil (Table 17).

Brazil's research and development program and military export plans began to show results in 1975. Under license and coproduction agreements, Brazil was manufacturing relatively unsophisticated conventional arms while importing modern sophisticated weaponry. As its export capacity increased, Brazilian arms imports increased. This relationship between arms imports and exports was part of a complex military industry on which Brazil began to depend in order to resolve its trade balance problems. According to this scheme, the military industry would generate a surplus that could be exported. The earnings from these exports would be invested in more modern armaments, which could in turn be used as models in the process of increasing Brazil's level of military technology. As this industry was based fundamentally on internal military expenditures, the evolution of the import-export scheme would directly reflect increases in the military budget.

Following the Anglo-Argentine Malvinas conflict, Brazil became more aware of its weaknesses vis-à-vis any potential extracontinental opponents. This has led Brazil to emphasize even further the modernization of both internally produced and imported arms. Brazil's decision to invest billions to modernize its navy illustrates this point.[16]

PERCEPTIONS OF THE SECURITY CONTEXT: HYPOTHESES AND PROPOSITIONS

The preceding analysis of the principal Latin American cases has revealed certain fundamental aspects of perceptions of threat and security. In this context, "security" is defined as the liberty to maintain and develop principal national values and interests within the overall international context. The security context is defined by each state's perception of national values and interests.

Hypothesis 1

My first hypothesis is that the security context depends upon all the international elements that each state perceives as affecting its potential to realize these values and interests. In the case of Cuba, the state broadened its conception of security context to include political-ideological factors and extraregional agents.

Proposition 1: Because the security context is defined by the state, it is necessary to define for each region, subregion, and country the type and nature of the elements that compose interdependent security systems.

Hypothesis 2

Based on the analysis of the cases of Central America and Cuba, my second hypothesis is that the security context depends upon how each state perceives its position in the interdependent system. This underscores the state's perception of its own willingness to act within that security context, whether politically, economically, diplomatically, or militarily.

Proposition 2: The actions of a state within a previously defined security context depend in part upon its approach to that security context. We must therefore study these approaches, specifying each state's goals, values, and interests.

Hypothesis 3

A third hypothesis derived from the analysis of both the Central American and Southern Cone cases is that security context also depends upon each state's perception of the degree of internal agreement (intranational elements) regarding the whole interdependent security system. Each state will view the external effect of alterations in internal relations differently.

Proposition 3: As each security context depends on the interaction and weight acquired by internal elements, we must determine how these internal events affect the international context of each state.

Hypothesis 4

The fourth hypothesis is that the security context is defined by each state's perception of the balance and reciprocal interaction between elements which are internal and external to its own security. As long as there is a perception of balance, the security context will not require compensations by arms.

Proposition 4: Because each security context depends upon a state's perception of the interaction and balance between internal and external elements, we must examine cases where this balance is upset to identify the methods that states adopt to reestablish the balance, putting special emphasis on the response of an arms buildup.

Hypothesis 5

A fifth hypothesis linked particularly to the case of Venezuela is that the security context depends upon each state's perception of variable international space. Following the temporary withdrawal of the United States from the Central American and Caribbean region, Venezuela perceived new space and therefore amplified its role, deepening its presence in the area and adapting its military potential to the redefined interdependent system.

Proposition 5: Because the security context of each state depends upon its perception of possible space in the respective security context, we must study both the willingness and the possibility of states to fill vacuums left by the withdrawal of other actors from the system.

Hypothesis 6

The sixth and final hypothesis, which emerges from the analysis of the case of Brazil, is that once a certain degree of arms buildup is achieved, the security context of a state encourages it to shift from increasing its stock of weapons quantitatively to improving those weapons qualitatively. A state that has already acquired a large supply of arms can maintain its strength only by improving the quality or sophistication of its weapons. Such pressures influence military powers of a second or third order.

Proposition 6: When the security context of states that have built a sizable arms supply impels them to make qualitative improvements, we must analyze the perceptions that particular states have of the trade-off between quantitative jumps (production under license and coproduction) and qualitative jumps (improved technology).

These hypotheses and propositions contain elements that may be incorporated into more or less coherent models. This, however, will depend fundamentally on the value of the research yet to be done. Due to the diversity of elements affecting security contexts, we need to systematize principal suppositions on which a useful model can be based. Although most states share a generic rationality, this may not be extended to all situations. Undoubtedly, each state constructs some rational relationship between desired ends and determined means. At this level, perhaps all share the same type of rationality. However, when confronted by particular signs and actions of opposing states, the contradictions between supposedly common rationalities are insurmountable.

Models of "shared rationality" are, in reality, not possible. Generic rationality must be limited to the assessment of means and ends. Internal and external events or signs are interpreted and evaluated very differently by states as they assess reinforcements or threats to their security contexts. At this level there is an implicit substantive rationality that causes each state to react differently to the events relevant to the given security context. National and international events are not interpreted similarly by all states. They do not convey objectively unequivocal meanings, nor produce reactions that may be considered "correct" or "flawed." All events are subject to interpretation by states within their particular security contexts, and subject as well to preexisting frameworks of interpretation. As B. Whaley states, "more than one hypothesis can, of course, be erected upon any given set of sensory inputs. This is a logical requirement of scientific hypothesis-building in general, but each specific builder (brain) has its own bias."[17]

Models of interpretation must therefore allow us to specify the particular biases of each state that affect evaluations and reactions to international events and internal affairs, or to the complex relationship between both. These models of interpretation, although subjective and broadly shared, are not necessarily conscious or formalized. Even the characterization of different frameworks of interpretation could be further analyzed. Models of perceptions and interpretations of security or danger may best be tested when a state is making a decision on defense. At this time, the frameworks of interpretation (or rationalities) of those who monopolize the decision-making process will be fundamental in determining the course of events.

To the degree that such frameworks permit a given evaluation of national and international affairs, they define the role and function that each element of a security context will play. From this standpoint, a cognitive model generates a particular collective sense of security. It is in this sense that Senghaas states that

> the external orientation is a relationship of deterrence that is just as *real* as it is *fictitious*, since the conflicts which one foresees with this enemy are formulated to a great extent on one's own side of the frontline. Although the deterrence system gives the appearance of extreme interdependence and foreign orientation, it is the expression of incomparable encapsulation and isolation with regard to the essential components.[18]

The strategic autism that Senghaas perceives in the relations of the superpowers can also be found within relations in underdeveloped areas such as Latin America. Because security systems are interdependent structures, one could say à la Boudon that the security systems in Latin America resemble the interdependent structure of state units as well.

Finally, because states utilize diverse frameworks of interpretation and configuration and because their definitions of security vary according to who monopolizes decision-making, it is possible to locate variations that coincide with distinct social types. One could establish particular models of interpretation according to who monopolizes decision-making. Different interpretive frameworks would tend more or less toward aggressive, offensive interpretations or toward a more pacifist or neutral orientation. At the level of defense policies in Latin America, interpretative frameworks utilized in decision-making must be redefined to allow nonmilitary or nonaggressive reactions to changes in security contexts.

NOTES

1. Cited in Anatol Rapoport, *Fights, Games and Debates* (Ann Arbor: University of Michigan Press, 1960), p. 35.

2. M. D. Wallace, "Old Nails in New Coffins: The Para Bellum Hypothesis Revisited," *Journal of Peace Research,* no. 1 (1981).

3. Anatol Rapoport, "Strategic Thinking in Theoretical Perspective" (typescript, 1980), p. 28b.

4. Ibid., p. 28a.

5. James W. Burton, *System, State Diplomacy and Rules* (New York: Cambridge University Press, 1968), p. 66.

6. Robert Jervis, "Hypothesis on Misperceptions," *World Politics,* April 1968, p. 475.

7. Robert Jervis, *Perceptions and Misperceptions in International Politics* (Princeton, N.J.: Princeton University Press, 1976), pp. 31–100. Quote on p. 90.

8. Alan L. George, D. K. Hall, and W. E. Simons, *The Limits of Coercitive Diplomacy* (Boston: Little, Brown, 1974), p. 526.

9. Alan L. George and R. Smoke, *Deterrence in American Foreign Policy* (New York: Columbia University Press, 1971), p. 215.

10. Bruce Russett, *Power and Community in World Politics* (San Francisco: W.H. Freeman, 1974), pp. 208–210.

11. Raymond Boudon, *La logique du social* (Paris: Hachette, 1979), p. 96.

12. See Russett, *Power and Community,* pp. 208–210.

13. George Kohler, "Toward a General Theory of Armaments," *Journal of Peace Research,* no. 2 (1979).

14. James L. Weaber, "Arms Transfers to Latin America: A Note on the Contagion Effect," *Journal of Peace Research,* no. 3 (1974).

15. Helan Jaworski, "Peru: La política internacional del gobierno militar peruano en dos vertientes (1968 a 1980)" (Paper presented at the seminar, Políticas exteriores latinoamericanas, Viña del Mar, Chile, September 1982), p. 52.

16. Augusto Varas, "El neuvo armamentismo latinoamericano: Consecuencia de la guerra de las Malvinas," *APSI,* no. 110 (July 1982).

17. B. Whaley, "Toward a General Theory of Deception," *Journal of Strategic Studies,* March 1982, p. 182.

18. Dieter Senghaas, "Toward an Analysis of Threat Policy in International Relations," in Klaus von Beyme, ed., *German Political Studies,* vol. 1 (London: Sage Publications, 1974), p. 75.

7. Military Conflicts and Regional Peace Agreements

The ineffectiveness of the mechanisms of conflict resolution between Latin American countries was dramatized in 1981 by the armed confrontation between Ecuador and Peru, in 1982 by the Anglo-Argentine conflict over the Malvinas, and in 1983 by the "secret war" of the United States against Nicaragua. Because of the presence of significant regional military powers on this continent, there has been renewed concern over the causes of such confrontations.

According to our previous analysis, to achieve a stable system of conflict resolution in Latin America, U.S. intervention in the region must be reduced, internal forces for democracy must be mobilized, and greater participation of the citizenry in the control of the armed forces and in the decision-making process must be promoted.

DISARMAMENT AND ARMS CONTROL PROPOSALS AND AGREEMENTS

Before World War II, Latin American governments set forth a variety of arms limitations proposals and agreements. In 1902 Argentina, Brazil, and Chile signed the "Pactos de Mayo," a disarmament agreement that compelled resale of some ships previously ordered by Argentina to Japan and by Chile to the United Kingdom. In 1923 Latin American ministries of foreign affairs made a joint declaration to prevent armed conflict between Latin American nations. A similar declaration was signed by all Latin American countries in 1933, and in 1936 the Conference on Peace Consolidation adopted a recommendation to limit the arms race in the region. After World War II, through the Interamerican Reciprocal Assistance Treaty (1947) and the Bogota Pact (1948), Latin American governments pledged not to use force in inter-American relations whenever a peaceful solution to conflict was available. They also created a continental assistance plan to aid individual countries in the event of an armed attack. Latin American governments[1] have participated recently in a number of global and regional arms limitation agreements, both nuclear and conventional (Tables 18 and 19).

The relatively minor participation of Latin American countries in arms limitation proposals contrasts starkly with the damaging effects of the arms race in the region. According to the available data, only three Latin American countries can be considered *active* parties in arms limitation proposals. Brazil and Mexico have joined in the presentation of most of the main proposals at the United Nations, and Argentina has supported some of them. The other Latin American countries have remained rather distant from disarmament and arms control initiatives and have been, at the most, passive elements. Even the active countries have a record of contradictory policies toward disarmament and arms limitation. This is true of Argentina, Brazil, Colombia, Peru, and Venezuela, which have supported general and complete disarmament yet are also the main forces within the regional arms race.

Most Latin American governments react similarly when faced with disarmament proposals. At the 1974 Ayacucho meeting, various Latin American countries agreed to a general declaration on disarmament, but never implemented its recommendations. Argentina's informal support for disarmament and arms limitation agreements is not matched by actual participation in these agreements. Argentina has ratified only two of seven major postwar accords: the Antarctic Treaty, through which it hopes to freeze the conflict with Chile and Brazil over this area, and the Outer Space Treaty. Three small Latin American countries—Panama, Nicaragua, and the Dominican Republic—have signed and ratified the Sea Bed Treaty. Disagreements about problems of maritime jurisdiction, however, have undermined support for this treaty. Argentina, Brazil, and Chile have consistently refused to ratify nuclear disarmament agreements. All three desire to keep control of all options for nuclear weaponry. Chile has, in fact, started a nuclear research and development program in recent years.

Recent nuclear policies in Peru may be explained in light of nuclear developments in Argentina, Brazil, and Chile. Peru has ratified the main regional denuclearization agreement, but, impelled by nuclear development in the other Southern Cone countries, it has accepted Argentine technological and scientific support to create a nuclear research and development program of its own. Concern over nuclear balance in the area threatens to set off a small-scale nuclear race.

A similar pattern emerged following the meeting of experts after the Ayacucho summit. In the 1974 Declaration of Ayacucho, Bolivia, Venezuela, Panama, Argentina, Colombia, Chile, and Ecuador agreed to limit armaments and promote peace and order. There were two subsequent meetings of experts to pursue these goals. The first was in Lima, Peru, in February 1975, and the second in Santiago, Chile, in September that same year. At the second meeting, a task force was appointed to develop a proposal for disarmament and arms limitation in the Andean area. A list of forbidden weapons was created, but it has been impossible to reach an agreement thus far.[2]

TABLE 18
Latin American Proposals and Declarations on Arms Limitation and Disarmament[a]

	General and Complete Disarmament	Cessation of Nuclear Weapons Tests	Nonproliferation of Nuclear Weapons	Nuclear Weapon-free Zones	Preventing Arms Race on the Sea Bed
Argentina	2			1	1
Bolivia				2	
Brazil	3	4	4	3	1
Chile	2			2	
Colombia	2				
Costa Rica			1		
Dominican Republic					
Ecuador				2	
El Salvador					
Guatemala					
Haiti					
Honduras					
Jamaica			1		
Mexico	8	4	4	3	3
Nicaragua					
Panama					
Paraguay					
Peru	1				
Trinidad and Tobago	1				
Uruguay					
Venezuela	1				

[a]Does not include signed treaties.

Source: Data derived from United Nations, Report of the Preparatory Committee for the Special Session of the General Assembly Devoted to Disarmament, vol. 5 (New York: UN, 1978).

Although the 1974 Declaration of Ayacucho had no real effects, its fundamental principles were reiterated in the joint communiqué of several Latin American foreign ministers in 1978. In this document the countries expressed their willingness to explore the reduction of conventional arms in the region. A similar initiative was taken in August 1978, when representatives of twenty Latin American and Caribbean countries signed a declaration on conventional disarmament and called upon the rest of the countries in the region to collaborate in this direction. Participants in this meeting also discussed the possibility of more specific consultations regarding the limitation of arms considered excessively harmful or having indiscriminate effects. Likewise, the possibilities of recommending measures to restrict trade of such armaments within the region were posed. Finally, in September 1980, Colombia, Costa Rica, Ecuador, Panama,

Preventing Arms Race in Outer Space	Chemical and Bio-logical Weapons	Environ-mental Warfare	Military Budgets	Arms Transfers	Declaration of Ayacucho
	2				x
				1	x
1	3		1		
					x
				1	x
				1	x
				1	
2	4	1			
					x
				1	
					x
				1	x

and Venezuela agreed upon a Charter of Conduct that called for a peaceful resolution to controversies and reiterated the principles of the Declaration of Ayacucho. In that same year, measures of mutual confidence included joint naval, land, and air maneuvers between diverse countries. Foreign dignitaries were invited to observe these maneuvers.

In sum, then, there is a widening gap between disarmament and arms limitation agreements, global or regional, and actual disarmament measures. Government policies in this matter are defined mostly by the military, particularly in matters relating to national strategies and specific inter-American political contingencies. Because of other priorities in national policies, we see a relative failure to implement disarmament and arms limitation measures. This contrasts with the "success" of the

TABLE 19
Ratification of Major Post-World War II Agreements by Latin American Countries

				Treaties			
	Antarctic	Partial Test Ban	Outer Space	Tlatelolco	Non-Proliferation	Sea Bed	Biological Warfare
Argentina	1961	--	1969	--	--	--	--
Bolivia	--	1966	--	1969	1970	--	1975
Brazil	1975	1965	1969	1968[a]	--	--	1973
Chile	1961	1965	--	1974[a]	--	--	--
Colombia	--	--	--	1972	--	--	--
Costa Rica	--	1967	--	1969	1970	--	1973
Dominican Republic	--	1964	1968	1968	1971	1972	1973
Ecuador	--	1964	1969	1969	1969	--	1975
El Salvador	--	1965	1969	1968	1972	--	--
Guatemala	--	1964	--	1970	1970	--	1973
Haiti	--	--	--	1969	1970	--	--
Honduras	--	1964	--	1968	1973	--	--
Jamaica	--	--	1970	1969	1970	--	1975
Mexico	--	1963	1968	1967	1969	--	1974
Nicaragua	--	1965	--	1968	1973	1973	1975
Panama	--	1966	--	1971	1977	1974	1974
Paraguay	--	--	--	1969	1970	--	1976
Peru	--	1964	--	1969	1970	--	--
Trinidad and Tobago	--	1964	--	1970	--	--	--
Uruguay	--	1969	1970	1968	1970	--	--
Venezuela	--	1965	1970	1970	1975	--	--

[a]Brazil and Chile have ratified the Treaty of Tlatelolco, but the treaty is not yet in force for either state, as both have refused to waive the requirements laid down in Article 28.

Source: Derived from SIPRI, Arms Control (London: Taylor and Francis, 1978).

regional arms race, which has driven regional military expenditures to more than US$18 billion in 1982.

CONTROL OF CONFLICTS AND FOREIGN POLICY

Initiatives intended to control conflicts in Latin America have had meager results. A general cause that is valid for every Latin American country is the autonomy their respective armed forces have acquired in defining defense policy and acquiring the means and mechanisms to carry it out. The military tends to scorn diplomatic resolutions to conflict and international political alliances, and to overestimate the potential of force to guarantee adequate external and internal security. Once defense policies are infused with this view, the context of security for each Latin American country comes to depend more and more strictly on the way that its own armed forces perceive and define security.

A recurring characteristic of the military's definition of a security context is the linking of foreign policy to the internal sociopolitical situation in each country. In South America, foreign policy is involved indissolubly in the strategy of civilian submission to the military. Foreign policy becomes indeed a dependent variable in this configuration of policy. In military relations, the perception that one armed force has of another is strongly determined by the nature and ideological orientation of the respective governments. Of great significance is the increased autonomy of the armed forces from the rest of the state. International political-military initiatives are strongly affected by the historical constitution of domestic military elements in each particular case. Given this high degree of military autonomy, each armed force defines its own security context, beginning with indigenous factors and including their position within the intraregional international situation.

Colombia

Colombia confronts great difficulties in the internal political arena because of the active presence of several national guerrilla groups. The extent of the armed action of the M-19 and the armed branch of the Colombian Communist Party (FARC, Revolutionary Armed Forces of Colombia) is unique on the continent. Unlike restricted guerrilla outbreaks in Venezuela, the Colombian guerrilla movement is a constant destabilizing force for local politics. The armed forces have undertaken an expensive program of military purchases to confront this internal threat, including the purchase of armored vehicles, automatic rifles, submachine guns, and TOW launchers.

Along with this buildup of war materiel for imposing internal order, the Colombian navy has incorporated ships and submarines purchased from Germany. This strengthening of naval power is oriented particularly toward the defense of Colombian territorial claims against Nicaragua in the Caribbean. Although Colombia politically supported the Sandinista revolution, the Nicaraguan claim to the San Andres Islands has injected a note of tension into relations between the two countries. The expansion of the Central American conflict and the anticipated eventual crisis in the Canal Zone have inclined Colombia to define its internal and external security context as one unit. Colombian security planners associate the internal guerrilla threat with the ideological-political support given to the guerrillas by Nicaragua.

Because of these interlocking internal and external conflicts, Colombia has pursued two different approaches. The first emphasized military solutions to all problems and downplayed diplomacy and negotiation. It also stressed Colombia's close ties with the United States and its support of the so-called Central American Democratic Community. Within this orientation, the Colombian government launched an offensive against the M-19 guerrilla movement. The second approach began with the election of President Betancur, who holds a different view of internal and external tensions. He initiated a peaceful settlement of the insurgency, including amnesty for the guerrillas, and has actively supported the Contadora Group in its efforts toward peace in Central America. Because of this change, Colombia has detached its regional policy from the United States and has followed a model more propitious to the negotiated settlement of international problems. Nonetheless, its armed forces maintain some important internal political leverage.

Ecuador and Peru

A different pattern has emerged in Ecuador, where the military is almost completely autonomous. After a long period of military governments of diverse types, the Ecuadorian armed forces, taking advantage of the oil bonanza, began to make major arms purchases and to increase military spending. The democratization that was initiated in Ecuador simultaneously did not jeopardize the autonomy of the armed forces; rather, it left them free to define the goals and appropriate tools of national defense. Thus, despite a new democratic government, the Ecuadorian armed forces were able to engage in a military campaign against Peru in 1981, repeating the war they lost in 1942 over Amazon territory. Whoever initiated the conflict, the recently installed democratic governments in both Ecuador and Peru were unable to prevent the confrontation.

The Peruvian response to the Ecuadorian military presence on its northern border was to deploy arms and mobilize its reserves nationally. Given the difference in size between the military forces of the two countries, the potential Ecuadorian threat to Peruvian territory was not substantial. Of particular significance is the fact that in both countries the initial confrontation and response were fundamentally military affairs, directed by the military high commands. In both countries, the recently elected civilian governments could only support mobilization and could not act effectively through diplomatic or multilateral channels such as the Organization of American States or the Andean Pact. This same situation was repeated in 1982 during the Malvinas conflict, when the Peruvian government tried to encourage political and diplomatic negotiations. Again, the armed forces emphasized military solutions and gave military aid to Argentina. Here the contradictions between perceptions of regional reality by the civilian government and the armed forces was shown in all its magnitude.

Furthermore, contradictions between the civilian government and the armed forces replicated the relations that had characterized the two former military governments. Under Velasco Alvarado and Morales Bermudez, the Peruvian foreign ministry reflected the will of the military in determining foreign policy. With the election of President Belaunde Terry, however, there was a gap between the foreign ministry and the armed forces. For these reasons, Belaunde's intention of being an active president and promoting international negotiation did not go over well in the foreign ministry and was blocked by the complete autonomy of the armed forces.

Both Ecuador and Peru, and to some extent Colombia, therefore show that the autonomy of military institutions is unimpeded by the existence of a civilian democratic government that has not achieved complete control of internal politics. When facing weak governments, the armed forces can continue independently of presidential orders.

The Effect of Military Autonomy

The most noteworthy case of military autonomy is that of the Argentine armed forces in the 1982 Malvinas conflict. When the military government of Leopoldo Galtieri became increasingly isolated from a social and political base of support, historical tendencies toward a "heterodox autonomy"[3] became associated with a counterfeit nationalism with strong chauvinist elements. The weak military government hoped that reliance on old nationalist theses would be the means to recuperate its position in the internal order.

Related lessons may be derived from the way in which Chile and Peru have attempted to resolve Bolivia's demand for an outlet to the sea. In 1977, when Chile and Peru both had military governments, they initiated discussions on a sea outlet for Bolivia. Chile had not touched upon the subject since the signing of the Lima Treaty in 1929. The rhetoric of both military governments, though it appeared to present a commitment to resolve Bolivia's landlocked position, nonetheless hid political calculation and contained self-serving geopolitical and military considerations. The Chilean proposal of a passage for Bolivia to the sea, although it did not contradict the terms of the 1929 treaty, was made without conducting previous diplomatic consultations with Peru, for which reason the latter reacted with deep reservations. Peru formulated a counterproposal that was unacceptable to Chile, since the internationalization of the sea outlet for Bolivia only delayed the question and did not resolve the problem thoroughly. In this way, both military governments ostensibly catered to Bolivia in the hope of neutralizing the other. Bolivia found its demand for an outlet to the sea delayed once again, with a Chilean-Peruvian conflict still pending.

A potential solution to Bolivia's landlocked situation was squandered due to considerations peculiar to the governing armed forces that subordinated viable political goals to purely tactical military ones. A similar pattern has characterized Argentine behavior in the conflict over the Beagle Channel. Argentina rejected the 1977 British arbitration and prepared to impose its view through the force of arms. Subsequently papal mediation was likewise questioned by the Argentine military government, which tried to take advantage of a favorable conjunction of military forces and diplomatic circumstances to isolate Chile and force it to cede its juridical position.

In sum, the intrusion of military considerations in the affairs of Latin American countries tends to limit and distort possible diplomatic or negotiated solutions to conflicts. These are replaced by solutions that rely on force or are otherwise obstructed by considerations of a military nature.

Recent evidence, however, indicates that internal political factors can revise retrograde foreign policies and encourage negotiated settlements of armed conflicts.

The Venezuela Case

Venezuela has historically favored disarmament initiatives and arms control and has enhanced its international standing in recent years through its oil and imaginative diplomacy. Nevertheless, some recent Venezuelan developments do not augur well for moderation in the arms field. Venezuela has recently increased its military spending and arms imports, and in its effort to modernize its armed forces, has put special emphasis on a supposed Cuban threat in Central America and the Caribbean. In association with the United States, it has favored armed opposition to revolutionary activities in the region. This policy has been reinforced by the presence of the Christian Democrat José Napoleón Duarte in El Salvador, who remained in power until 1982 and received the full support of Venezuela's counterpart governing party, the Christian Democratic Party of Venezuela (COPEI). When Venezuela's claims on the Essequibo region of Guyana are added to its policies on Central America, the country gives the impression of being more concerned with military solutions than political or diplomatic negotiations.

In the recent past, two important events show how the relationship between the internal situation and foreign policy can produce different results according to how they interact. The electoral defeat of Duarte in El Salvador meant the erosion of domestic political support for the Venezuelan governing party, COPEI. Since the political formula attempted by Herrera Campins failed and Duarte was replaced by an ultra-rightist, internal support of the COPEI foreign policy suffered and threatened to weaken its electoral support in 1983. Together with this failure of Venezuela's Central American policy, the government of Guyana took a hard-line reaction to Venezuela's demands for the Essequibo. This led the Christian Democrat government to seek Venezuelan incorporation into the nonaligned movement, effectively neutralizing nonaligned support for Guyana. These recent events have coincided with an economic and financial crisis in Venezuela that is likely to increase internal discontent and make management of the country increasingly difficult.

Although Venezuela had earlier sought to build up its military power in response to a confluence of internal and external factors, changes in these factors now incline Venezuela's rulers to opt for a more moderate policy of diplomatic initiatives. This moderate policy includes greater reluctance to associate with U.S. efforts to isolate Nicaragua in Central America, a less aggressive attitude toward Cuba, and a more stable political relationship with Mexico for cooperation in the area.

However, the reaction of the Venezuelan armed forces regarding this change of policy is as yet unknown. Other imponderables include the degree to which the armed forces would prefer military solutions to all conflicts and the degree to which they will insist on a larger budget, despite Venezuela's economic difficulties. If they are committed to armed solutions and large budgets, this could reverse the present policy tilt toward moderation. The recent initiative of Guyana to purchase weapons from Brazil similarly weakens negotiating tendencies in Venezuela over militarist options.

Brazil

Finally, the Brazilian case illustrates a pragmatic, international policy that favors negotiation over force. This is highly significant, considering that Brazil is the top military power in South America. Faced with various disputes and pressured by armed forces that perform a political function of primary importance, Brazil has nonetheless been able to act in the region in a nonconflictive though determined way. Numerous disputes with neighbors have been resolved through negotiation with each one of the countries in question. Especially in the case of Argentina, the Brazilian Foreign Ministry has tried to achieve joint cooperation agreements in the hydroelectric and nuclear areas.

The explanation of this apparent anomaly is found in the professionalism of Itamaraty, the Brazilian Foreign Ministry, which has been able to make its perspective prevail over that of the military.[4] This civilian control of Brazilian foreign policy is particularly striking in trade and financial relations with socialist countries. The civilian economic leadership in Brazil has neutralized the Brazilian military in that respect, in order to pursue broad agreements such as those established by the governmental and entrepreneurial mission headed by the minister of planning, Delfim Netto, to the Soviet Union in 1981.[5]

Nevertheless, one of the consequences of the 1982 Malvinas conflict could be the increased use of force in the resolution of controversies. For example, the Brazilian navy has observed with concern the presence of extracontinental powers in the South Atlantic. In the aftermath of the Malvinas conflict, Brazil's high command has increased pressure for greater budgets and accelerated naval modernization. As a result of this international situation, civilian-military tensions in Brazil may increase. Another factor that could present a greater margin for internal conflict is the ongoing process of political liberalization. As the opposition continues to gain popular support, the armed forces may feel that their position is threatened. Together with the post-Malvinas external situation, this could make a moderate negotiating position on the part of Itamaraty more difficult.

In synthesis, the probability of controlling interstate conflict in Latin America through diplomacy and foreign policies rests on several factors. It depends increasingly upon internal political conditions, especially on the capacity for civilian control over armed forces, as well as on the security context of each Latin American country. In a security situation perceived as favorable and in a situation of weak civilian control, the armed forces will impose their perspective of confrontation. On the contrary, if there is civilian control or if the security context of that country is seen by the armed forces as unstable, negotiating tendencies will emerge even when pressures for high military budgets are maintained.

U.S. POLICY TOWARD THE REGION

The strategic importance of Latin America has often been exaggerated, particularly by the Latin American armed forces themselves. From the mid-1950s until the beginning of the 1970s, the continent was of political and ideological importance to the United States, but it performed no strategic military functions.[6] Military relations between the region and the United States thus acquired a more ideological-political than strategic connotation. For the same reason, as soon as the political orientation of Latin American governments changed—Velasco in Peru, Allende in Chile, Juan José Torres in Bolivia, and Perón in Argentina—or when the orientation of the U.S. administration toward the region was modified—Carter and human rights, for example—the fragility of military relations with the United States was clear. The crisis of the so-called "Pan-American military system" at the beginning of the 1970s was a result, therefore, of the politicization and ideologization of the relations between Latin American and U.S. armed forces.

The crisis of Pan-American military relations during the Carter administration led countries with military governments, such as Argentina, Brazil and Chile, to terminate military ties in the face of U.S. pressure on human rights. Nevertheless, it was precisely during the period between 1976 and 1980 that Argentina and Chile received the greatest financial support from the United States.

With the administration of Ronald Reagan, a new stage has been initiated in military links between Latin America and the United States. The United States has tried to further its interests in the region through support for de facto governments, all of which are clearly oriented to the right and strongly repressive in internal matters. This has led to normalization of diplomatic and military links between the United States and right-wing dictatorships in Latin America.

Following the 1982 Malvinas conflict, renewed emphasis was placed on ties with Latin American armed forces. It was considered necessary to reestablish and improve Pan-American military relations in order to discourage extracontinental influence and, at the same time, assure the "governability" of those countries. In the Argentine case these factors overlapped. On the one hand, the armed forces were involved in an offensive military action that was not supported by the United States. On the other hand, the defeat of the Argentine armed forces quickened the return to civilian rule, which, from the U.S. view, tended to increase its ungovernability.

As a consequence, the role that the United States is likely to play in the region during the Reagan administration will demonstrate greater involvement in political-military matters, greater indifference to questions related to human rights, and greater attention toward matters of financial order or foreign debt. These characteristics point toward greater control of intraregional conflicts. This new orientation of U.S. policy contrasts with previous U.S. policies, which were less interventionist and less capable of managing conflicts in the region. This was demonstrated in the Chilean-Argentine crisis in 1978 and the Peruvian-Ecuadorian confrontation in 1981. This perspective of mounting involvement of the Reagan administration will be seen mainly in the smaller Latin American countries. It will not be possible in Brazil, which has already ceased to be a preferential ally of the United States in order to acquire an autonomous role in the region. Contradictions between the policies of these two countries may become a source of conflict, as Brazilian pragmatism may clash with U.S. interventionism.

TOWARD A LATIN AMERICAN POLICY
ON CONTROL OF CONFLICTS

Unfortunately, greater U.S. involvement in Latin America will mean greater U.S. capacity to monitor conflicts that may arise there. Besides threatening the Latin American states involved, a U.S.-directed system of control is not adapted to Latin American realities and hence creates a high level of volatility and instability. A system thus conceived can rest only on frustrated and dissatisfied military sentiments, which in any event would revive intraregional competition and sharpen conflicts.

A viable, stable system of conflict resolution implies some type of noninterventionist hemispheric commitment. Insofar as internal Latin American politics are concerned, democratically expressed civilian forces must have the real ability to control armed institutions. Development of an effective system of conflict control in Latin America requires that both conditions be met.

Assuming that these necessary but not sufficient conditions could be met, some additional general ideas may be expressed in order to elaborate a national policy of effective control of conflicts in the region. The building of confidence measures, which is a first step in decreasing intraregional tensions, should be complemented by a group of typically local measures that are oriented in the same direction but vary with the specific circumstances of each Latin American case.

For different internal political reasons, almost all Latin American countries have been incapable of subjecting their armed institutions to effective civilian control. A first measure toward ensuring peaceful resolution of conflict is to bring all armed institutions to civilian control by an executive selected on a legitimate representative basis. A unified civil command over the armed services is fundamental.

A second measure is to incorporate the civil sectors into mechanisms for conflict resolution at the regional level. For example, the mechanisms for conflict resolution within the Organization of American States, as well as potential mechanisms within the Andean Pact and Latin American Economic System (SELA), should be broadened to include existing nongovernmental organizations that have played an important role in reducing interstate tensions. We are referring to the Catholic Church, youth movements such as the Peace and Justice Service, labor organizations of all kinds, women's organizations, and other intellectual and cultural groups. All such groups have been historically isolated from decisions affecting conflict resolution, but their opinions are particularly relevant because their membership is composed of those principally affected by the increase in tensions. If such nongovernmental organizations were included in conflict resolution, popular participation in the search for peaceful and stable solutions could be institutionalized. In this respect, it is fitting to call attention to the important effort that intellectual, cultural, and Catholic groups made in Argentina and Chile in successfully containing the danger of war in 1978 over the Beagle Channel.

In all nations with unresolved boundary disputes, a popular consensus on border issues should be sought. This is particularly important for Peru and Chile regarding the acutely sensitive issue of Bolivia's demand for an outlet to the sea. To build a positive consensus will require overcoming Peru's reticence toward a solution that would include terminating its border dispute with Chile. A more reasonable diplomatic style of greater collaboration will also have to be promoted. More generally, consensus building would involve initiating negotiations at an academic and intellectual level that would not be binding and could therefore fabricate agreements potentially acceptable to all governments. As long as the autonomy of the Peruvian armed forces is not limited and Chile does not restore a fully democratic system, it will be very difficult to advance decisively in these matters. If civilian control is stabilized in Bolivia, this would facilitate initiation of tripartite meetings at the academic level toward resolution of this conflict.

Finally, in the cases of Venezuela and Brazil, positive tendencies that already exist in both countries must be reinforced through the aforementioned recommendations. State and multilateral mechanisms for conflict resolution must be opened to civilian participation and control. Together with the greater participation of nongovernmental institutions, consensus building must be emphasized. The new participation of Venezuela in organizations such as the nonaligned movement and the greater proximity of Brazil to intraregional organizations such as SELA and the Andean Pact could accelerate positive trends in both countries.

In summary, an effective system of conflict resolution depends upon the ability of Latin American countries to reduce U.S. intervention in the region, and requires a system of stronger intraregional alliances. It further depends on the complete rule of democracy in these countries as a necessary condition for the full participation of the citizenry and their control of the armed forces. Bilateral and multilateral governmental organizations responsible for resolving interstate conflicts should be reformed to include greater participation of nongovernmental organizations. Finally, there should be ample meetings, whether bilateral or multilateral, between those directly involved in the disputes and interested in peace. To the extent that these recommended mechanisms for conflict resolution promote popular participation in decision-making, democracy will be strengthened at the regional level and interstate conflicts, which are in large part due to narrow interests, will be contained.

NOTES

This is a revised version of Augusto Varas, "Controlling Conflict in South America: National Approaches," in Michael Morris and Victor Millán, eds., *Controlling Latin American Conflicts* (Boulder, Colo.: Westview Press, 1983).

1. It should be emphasized that this analysis focuses on South America, disregarding the situation in Central America.

2. Positions regarding the list of weapons to be limited or eliminated from Latin American arsenals vary in accordance with the strategic position and policies of these countries. As a result of these differences, a third meeting of experts never took place. At the first two meetings, consensus was reached on the prohibition of biological, chemical, toxic, and nuclear weapons; ballistic missiles; carriers; cruisers; and nuclear submarines. Regarding missile range, definite differences emerged between Colombia, Chile, and Ecuador, on the one hand, and Bolivia, Peru, and Venezuela, on the other. The former supported

prohibition of strategic missiles; the latter wanted to maintain this option and prohibit 50-km range missiles. Peru opposed the prohibition of artillery above 105mm. Colombia and Chile supported a ban on all type of bombers. Gerardo Cortés Rencoret, "Los tratados de armamentos en América," *Seguridad Nacional,* January-March 1978.

3. Juan Carlos Puig, "Política internacional Argentina" (Paper presented at the seminar, Políticas exteriores comparadas de América Latina, Caracas, October 4–6, 1982).

4. See Alexandre S. C. Barros, "The Formulation and Orientation of Brazilian Diplomacy" (Paper presented at the seminar, Comparative Latin American Foreign Policies, Viña del Mar, Chile, September 20–23, 1982).

5. See Augusto Varas, "Las relaciones de América Latina con la Unión Soviética: Los casos de Argentina, Brasil, Chile y Perú," (Paper presented at the seminar, Comparative Latin American Foreign Policies, Viña del Mar, Chile, September 20–23, 1982).

6. See James C. Haar, "Ayuda militar para la América Latina," *Military Review,* May 1969.

8. The Armed Forces and the Military Regime in Chile

Militarization and the arms race in Chile since 1973 are good examples of the situation analyzed above. The civilian-military insurrection in Chile on September 11, 1973, overthrew not only Chile's tradition of democracy, but also the myth of the historical subordination of the country's military to civilian power.[1] The Chilean armed forces had, in fact, given the impression of being removed from national politics for more than forty years. After the government of General Carlos Ibáñez (1927–1931), civilian powers segregated the armed forces from public life. The antimilitaristic political sentiment that followed Ibáñez's military government, coupled with the economic crisis of the 1930s, which severely hurt Chile's export-oriented economy, translated into a reduction of state funds for the military. This contradiction of the budget coincided with the political isolation of the armed forces, and the military was left to overcome its institutional problems on its own.

Adaptations between the military and the polity began in 1931. The armed forces submitted to civilian power, resisting coup attempts as well as the National Socialist conspiracy of 1938 and the aborted uprising of General Ariosto Herrera in 1939. Frequent putsches, as in 1952 and 1969, did not change the political position of the Chilean military.[2] In spite of low pay and a shortage of arms, the military did not challenge civilian rule.

In 1938, the armed forces began to support import-substitution industrialization. The Military Work Corps (Cuerpo Militar del Trabajo) were created to train recruits in the use of machinery and tools. The army pursued its own technical development by trying to lower its maintenance costs and by small-scale production of goods for barracks consumption.[3]

In spite of their lack of political participation, the armed forces also began to increase and diversify their linkages with other parts of the state and to assume institutional responsibility for activites not directly connected with national defense. These activities could very well have continued in civilian hands. In this way, the Chilean armed forces began a slow but systematic process of reentry into politics, which by 1973 covered such important (but far from inherently military) activities as transportation, communications, sports, and recreation.[4] The 1973 military insurrection, however, cannot be explained exclusively by this background. It must be placed within a broader national political and historical context. The weakening of military submission to civilian authority was one of the principal factors in unleashing the coup.

The exceptional nature of the Chilean case lies not so much in the actual subordination of the military to civilian authority, as in the *appearance* the armed forces gave of noninvolvement in politics and the total lack of perception by civilians of the actual weakness of their control over the armed forces. The military insurrection of 1973 must be situated within the general framework of the historical development of the Chilean armed forces. From this perspective we will analyze the political and military reasons for the coup; the political functions the armed forces currently carry out; the principal characteristics of the military's institutional development; and the prospects for change in the military government.

THE ARMED FORCES AND THE
CIVIL-MILITARY INSURRECTION

Three important features may be discerned in the institutional development of the Chilean armed forces prior to 1973. First, the supply of armaments was insufficient and the process of modernization was slow compared to the Peruvian and Argentine armed forces (neighboring countries with which there had been a history of tense, and sometimes conflictive, relations). Second, the pay of uniformed personnel was low.[5] Third, the military was continually involved in trying to alleviate the first two conditions.

These tensions exploded in October 1969, when General Roberto Viaux incited a regiment in the city of Santiago to mutiny, demanding improvement of the army's material conditions. This military rebellion was due, in part, to the historically low and decreasing allocation of state funds to the military, and in part to the growing gap between the Chilean armed forces and their Argentine and Peruvian confreres.

The political role of the military in Peru had increased significantly in 1962, when the armed forces stepped in temporarily to prevent the election of a leftist as president. Following the Velasco coup of 1968 and the outright establishment of a military government, the army's material resources improved considerably. Not only was the military budget increased, but the U.S. arms supply monopoly was also broken with the purchase of Mirage jets from France in 1968. The arms industry in Argentina had also developed significantly, and following the military coups in the 1960s and 1970s, the army could be sure of large and growing budgets.

The situation of the armed forces in both Peru and Argentina contrasted sharply with that in Chile. Restrictions on the military increased as neither the Eduardo Frei nor the Salvador Allende governments considered the military or the country's defense as supremely important issues. Neither government developed a comprehensive military policy. Civilian political forces approached problems of national defense from the point of view of peaceful negotiation. Army officers, on the other hand, were increasingly convinced of the importance of military preparedness and a stockpile of weapons to guarantee national defense. There was little effort to create a shared perspective.

Viaux's October 1969 movement did improve the material situation of the armed forces. From then on we note a significant increase in the military budget. The increase in the Chilean defense budget thus began *prior* to the 1973 coup, specifically after the 1969 insurrection. From that point, and including the period of the Popular Unity government (1970–1973), the military budget rose. Although it decreased during the 1975–1976 recession, it rose again (partly as a result of tensions with Argentina) in 1977. These data indicate that material and financial issues were not the principal factors behind the insurrection of the armed forces in 1973; other factors compelled the break with the democratic constitutional framework.

In the first place, it is important to point out that the September 1973 coup followed other unsuccessful attempts. These include the plots of generals Roberto Viaux and Camilo Valenzuela in October 1970; of General Alfredo Canales in 1972; and of the corporatist sectors in June 1973.

Although the coup was a successful civilian insurrection that was completed militarily by the armed forces, there were also some strictly military factors contributing to the coup. The army's high command, headed by General Carlos Prats, had not been able to find new sources of arms supplies. The United States had placed financial, political, and military embargoes[6] on President Allende's government that were accepted internationally. The Soviet Union was the only alternative source of arms. General Prats, then commander in chief of the army and minister of defense, toured socialist countries. This did not, however, result in a new source of arms supplies. Although arms were available at low interest rates and with long-term repayment from the Soviet Union (which also was supplying and continues to supply Peru), the Chilean high command was dissuaded from switching suppliers.

Within this context, the armed forces had two options: to continue giving political support to the Allende government and to accept its mechanisms of conflict resolution, or to switch its support to the side of the civilian insurrection and reestablish ties with the United States. Evidently the weakness of democratic constitutionalism within the armed forces kept them from choosing the democratic option, which would have meant less loss of life. Lacking a deep commitment to constitutionalism and democracy, the military chose a line of action that maintained and reinforced their conservative ideological and political characteristics.

In short, the political factors behind the armed forces' choice of insurrection included the weakness of their constitutional beliefs and values, pressures from the United States, the failure to switch arms suppliers, the crisis of legitimacy in the executive branch, and finally the confidence within the barracks that a coup could succeed.

THE POLITICAL FUNCTION OF THE ARMED FORCES
WITHIN THE MILITARY GOVERNMENT

The armed forces' political role in the military government will be considered in the following analysis within the context of the background given above. Options of economic and social policies will also be related to the broad political and class front that overthrew the Allende government.

One of the first elements in consolidating the role of the armed forces in government was establishing the leadership of the army's high command over the army and other branches of the military. Because the military coup was a joint effort of different branches of the armed forces, the situation after the coup was one of relative anomie. Having destroyed the previous normative political and legal order, the armed forces needed to reach an interinstitutional agreement that would guide their relations and positions *within* the government. During the junta's first year, lines of command were clarified and the primacy of the army over the other branches was established.

By June 1974 the leading role of the army had been consolidated. Its commander in chief, General Augusto Pinochet, became president of the republic. All the armed forces, including the Police Corps (Cuerpo de Carabineros) and the Bureau of Investigations (Direccion General de Investigaciones), were unified under the Ministry of Defense and became responsible to the president. The repressive forces were unified under the National Intelligence Agency (Direccion Nacional de Inteligencia), to be headed by a superior officer in active service named by the president. Thus the process of unifying the military command around the commander in chief of the army and the president of the republic (Pinochet occupied both positions) lasted for almost a year—a year of difficult tensions for the armed forces.

The apparent ease with which these tensions were resolved in favor of the army and its high command was due to the military's commitment to a vertical system of command. The professionalization of the Chilean armed forces was accomplished at the beginning of the twentieth century under the guidance of German officers. It was later complemented by military training from the United States starting with the Military Assistance Pact in 1952. These two processes of professionalization instilled a commitment to hierarchy and vertical command. As the political involvement of the several branches of the armed forces introduced the danger of conspiracy against the vertical hierarchy within and among them, the army's high command could utilize these principles to argue for the consolidation and fortification of its position within the government.

The army's high command achieved complete hegemony over its own branch, and then over the other branches of the armed forces. All superior officers (generals and admirals) who had partcipated in some way in the military insurrection were retired. This achieved two results simultaneously. Internal dissent was eliminated, opening the way for unchallenged leadership from the government. A generational break was also established between the commander in chief of the army and the staff of generals. The minister of defense had been a student of Pinochet in the Military School and his close aide during the military insurrection.[7] The marked generational difference between General Pinochet and the other superior officers reinforced his leadership over the entire military.

A second characteristic of the Chilean armed forces concerns the relation between the military as such and the governmental roles of certain officers appointed by the president. As the armed forces have not taken over government leadership in institutional terms, their branches can devote themselves to professional development, taking full advantage of the large budgets granted them by the military executive.

From a strictly institutional view of the management of national life, the armed forces cannot be said to have penetrated the state. Compared with the military's assumption of typically civilian responsibilities prior to the coup, it must be ceded that the military has decreased its possible institutional control of the state. In fact, it is only possible to discern small spheres of direct military institutional management of the political system, such as the participation of a representative of each branch of the armed forces (including the Police Corps) in the Chilean Copper Commission, the Copper Corporation, the Energy Commission, the Film Censorship Council, and the National Radio. As one can see from these examples, which cover almost the entirety of the armed forces' new institutional functions, direct institutional involvement of the armed forces in the political management of the country is quite limited.[8]

A clear separation has been established between the armed forces' relatively minor governmental functions and their military and defense functions. The continuing potential for international conflict, first with Peru and later with Argentina, has helped reinforce the tendency to segregate the armed forces from governmental management and to keep them from debating strictly governmental issues. General Pinochet's dual roles as commander in chief of the armed forces and president of the republic have been strengthened by this institutional distance, which is replicated within each branch of the armed forces. The separation is associated with two features of the regime: the president's great autonomy in governing, and the role he has taken in conflicts within the regime.

Executive autonomy is buttressed by the fact that any criticism within the military of governmental leadership would constitute a direct questioning of the vertical command and internal hierarchy so highly valued by its members. Therefore the executive has the capacity to modify, accelerate, or eliminate any public policy, and may count on the permanent support of the armed forces. Pinochet has thus been able to overcome all of the crises he has faced without any substantial changes of government authorities.

It is instructive to compare Chile's political-military situation with that of the Argentine and Brazilian military governments, which have had periodic changes of the head of state. In Argentina and Brazil, the armed forces have themselves assumed the responsibility of governing, even when they delegate the presidency to one or another of their members. In these cases, the executive head renounces his position as commander in chief of the army. (The Argentine president, General Galtieri, was exceptional in retaining his military position.) This pattern has advantages and disadvantages for military regimes. On the one hand, in regimes where the armed forces rule institutionally, there is a flexibility and an ease in changing policies, which means that errors may be corrected and policy directions changed without high political costs. In the Chilean case, on the contrary, a change in the orientation of policies to which the president has been strongly committed would imply a major crisis within the armed forces. On the other hand, the Chilean regime has shown a greater capacity for leadership in comparison with situations characterized by dispersion and incoherence of leadership. This latter problem contributed to the fall of Argentine president Roberto Viola and his replacement by General Galtieri, commander in chief of the Argentine army.

Finally, the concentration of political-military power, as in Chile, offers less of an opportunity for stability and long-range solidification of the military regime. With the concentration of power, duties are not delegated, broad social and political support is not mobilized, and the regime therefore lacks solid social foundations. This situation contrasts, for example, with the Brazilian case. There the armed forces have institutional responsibilities in governing, and at the same time have developed political organizations that open the political system to competition. A scheme of this type would be unthinkable within the Chilean regime. Although the Chilean political system is characterized by a dictatorship *composed of* military officers, it is not a government *of* the armed forces. The nature of the executive role in the system explains the changes and tensions Chile is currently undergoing.

Another aspect of the current Chilean regime is the executive's considerable autonomy relative to the armed forces supporting the regime. As political and military power is concentrated in the presidency, that person becomes an important factor in the stability of the regime. Pinochet is arbiter of the tensions and disputes among supporting civilian factions and does not obey a particular internal combination of those factions. This arbitration of the president has helped to hold together the heterogeneous political bloc that is still governing. This bloc is composed of the armed forces, corporatist interest groups, entrepreneurs, and technocrats who followed neoconservative economic policies. Contradictions within this political alliance are resolved definitively by the executive, who has the authority to allocate resources and dictate policies.

These features of executive autonomy, arbitration, and concentration of power enhance the regime's capacity to dominate and implement government policies. These same features, however, are also sources of instability. Because the regime rests fundamentally on the loyalty of the armed forces to the government, any large crisis in "the model" or modification in the domination within the armed forces would make the regime precarious. Consequently, although the regime does possess instruments of political stability, its capacity to solidify its position in the long run is increasingly questionable, as was seen in 1984 when the government proved unable to cope with social unrest through political means.

The regime is furthermore ideologically impotent. This must be seen within the context of the ideological and doctrinal development of the armed forces, which has included the accumulation of values that have been translated into a national security doctrine. This doctrine explains extramilitary social behavior from a military point of view, addressing the armed forces' increasing concern about and involvement in national life. The military justifies and legitimates its coup on the basis of national security principles that transform internal political dissidents into enemies who must be forcefully repressed. Nevertheless, to the extent that the armed forces have *not* become privileged policy-makers, their capacity to propagandize Chilean society is reduced and their ideological function checked.

The armed forces' national security doctrine simply cannot compete ideologically with stronger and more coherent values. It is opposed by a market ideology that argues the need to liberalize the entire economy (and therefore implicitly the entire society) by removing all state interference and control. Government policies are thus oriented to limit state participation in all economic and social activities—except for repressive ones. Supporters of this market ideology include Nobel Prize winning economist Milton Friedman as well as the international center of economic neoconservatism—the Economics Department of the University of Chicago. It also has supporters within the Chilean government's economic technocracy.

Given the strength of the market ideology, the ability of the national security doctrine to permeate Chilean society is questionable. Additionally, the national security doctrine includes several elements that contradict the market ideology. Historically, the Chilean armed forces have been state oriented and have struggled for greater participation, through the state, in public life. As the antistatist, free-trade, free-market, and monetarist model was imposed, the ideology of national security was left with no state policies to support. As a set of values, it has become completely isolated from the main transformations Chilean society has undergone.

The doctrine of national security was further challenged by the "sub-ideology" of the consumer society, which implicitly accepted and glorified the goals of the market ideology. Pseudo-values of consumption and material wealth permeate Chilean society, strengthened by the commercial media, which inundate the country with false images of abundance and consumption. Against this popular glorification of the consumer society, the military was impotent to impose its new ideology. The basic values of the officers did not correspond to the role of transforming society; they did not intend to undertake this function and the government has been unable to carry it out. All this ultimately translated into a deep ideological crisis in the armed forces within Chilean society.

In summary, although the armed forces provide the main support for the regime, they do not participate directly in government leadership. This has negative consequences on the stability of political-military domination and on the diffusion of military values throughout the rest of society. The armed forces are subordinate to the state technocracy in guiding the transformations of society, and they are reduced to carrying out the functions of external defense and internal repression. This situation has encouraged the armed forces to establish new relationships with civilians, as described below.

PRINCIPAL FEATURES OF MILITARY INSTITUTIONAL DEVELOPMENT

The institutional support that the armed forces give to the regime exists within an economic and social "model" that contradicts the traditional military project for the remaking of Chilean society. If one could construct an ideal type of military socioeconomic project for the country, its diverse elements would be found within the institutional development of the armed forces. The first element could be found within the military government of General Ibáñez (1927–1931). During this period the material and institutional conditions for the industrial development of the country were established. Throughout this process the military favored strong state participation in the economy, especially in public works, public investment, and social services. It also backed protectionist measures to stimulate an increasingly important industrial sector, which eventually replaced the traditional agricultural *latifundio* as the major force in Chile's economy. Subsequently, during their long political isolation, the armed forces supported the general strategy of import substitution industrialization, encouraging state economic action together with private initiative.

Along with the process of gradual reentry into political and state life, these elements of the armed forces' historical identity (corroborated by their own institutional self-description) provide the elements of an ideal type of socioeconomic development, which could be described as authoritarian industrialist capitalism. The capitalist component lies in the armed forces' critical allegiance to the capitalist organization of production. Even during the short-lived "Socialist Republic" of June 1932, in which some sectors of the military participated, the "socialist" character stemmed from the magnitude of state economic activity and intervention in national life. The Chilean armed forces have been characterized by a procapitalist orientation, although they have simultaneously tried to smooth the rough edges and keep workers' aspirations in check. Their anticommunism precedes the Russian Revolution and is a reaction instead to the anarchist leadership of the Chilean workers' movement. This has prevented them from adopting a very radical position for change.

The military's support for industrialization and for the involvement of the state in the economy may be explained not only in terms of their historical practice, but also in terms of ideological influences. The "Prussian ideology," for example, was instilled by the German instructors of the modern Chilean army. This ideology values industrialization and associates military and industrial development. The armed forces' sense of the country's problems is shaped by such military ideologies and values. Armed forces that favor such orientations but lack the institutional means or political space to realize them may resort to authoritarian measures to ensure that their goals are achieved.

The authoritarian industrialist capitalism typical of the armed forces does not blend well with the neoconservative socioeconomic "model," which would remove the state from national economic activity. If the radical privatization of the first years of the military government contradicted the historical orientations of the armed forces, then why and how did they support this model?

I believe that the resolution of this apparent contradiction lies in the political events leading up to the crisis of 1973. The situation by September of that year was one of great political polarization, expressed through a civilian insurrection. The government appeared incapable of resolving the crisis. Inflation was soaring due to problems in production, wage and salary structures, and the international financial blockade against the Allende government.

At this juncture, for the armed forces to withdraw their support for the government implied the restriction of economic options. Economic stabilization and the containment of inflation would require a sharp reduction of the state's fiscal deficit, the sale of state enterprises to the private sector, and the freezing of wages and salaries. Economic stabilization within this context of the political option implied a strengthening of the more conservative and authoritarian ideological tendencies within the armed forces.

TABLE 20
Military and Educational Expenditures in Chile, 1973-1979 (1973=100)

Year	Total Fiscal Expenditures[a]	Military Expenditures	Educational Expenditures	Military Exp. as Percentage of Fiscal Exp.
1973	100.0	100.0	100.0	12.3
1974	68.5	136.0	107.1	29.1
1975	46.3	108.3	77.4	34.3
1976	47.2	107.5	87.9	33.3
1977	57.4	138.7	113.1	35.4
1978	66.8	155.8	128.5	34.2
1979	75.8	270.3	147.1	32.9

[a]Fiscal expenditure is a concept similar, but not identical, to the concept of "public expenditure." Both are indicators of state activity in the economy, but the former essentially measures the activity of administratively centralized institutions, while the latter includes the activity of decentralized institutions as well. During the 1970s, total fiscal expenditures have ranged from about 65% to 75% of total public expenditures. For more detail about these indicators, see Jorge Marshall, "Gasto público en Chile: 1969-1979," Estudios, no. 5 (July 1981).

Source: Documentation collected by FLACSO, Santiago.

This military economic policy, derived from the initial political option, further implied that the objective of industrialization would be subordinated to that of stabilization. Part of the stabilization program was carried out through the sale of state enterprises and state shares in joint ventures. The private sector, which had recently emerged from its 1970–1973 crisis, went into debt abroad in order to purchase state enterprises and stocks. Social capital was transferred to private hands with a strong connection to foreign finance. This was facilitated by the increase in international liquidity following the increase in OPEC oil prices. In brief, the construction of the neoconservative economic model can be seen, from the viewpoint of the armed forces, as a succession of interconnected options, each conditioned by the previous ones.

Both the governing bloc and its economic model were formed during this period. The governing bloc is composed of the politically dominant and repressive armed forces, monopolistic and oligarchic business sectors, transnational corporations, state technocrats, and corporatist apologists. The rest of the population is excluded not only from the decision-making process, but also from the benefits of the system, such as they are. Within this political and economic framework, the armed forces find that their institutional interests *may* coincide with the characteristics of the model followed by the technocrats. This model has included sharp reductions in public spending (as can be seen in Table 20), which have had positive institutional consequences for the military.

Privatization of the economy has included the reduction of state investment, the sale of state property, and the restriction of the role of the state in areas as important as public works, construction, housing, health, social security, agriculture, mining, industry, commerce, and energy. Although the gross national product has risen in recent years, public spending has increased at much lower levels. Within this context of reduced spending, only military and educational budgets have shown notable increases in both absolute and per capita terms during the 1973–1979 period. The former has increased much more rapidly than the latter. The increases in the military budget have been justified by critical border situations, initially in the north with Peru and later in the south with Argentina, and by repressive activities (the figures in Table 21 include spending on the Police Corps and Bureau of Investigations). These increases in defense spending have absorbed a good part of the state's resources formerly allocated to economic investment and public services such as health and housing.

The privatization of the economy has meant that state expenditures were cut by more than half in the two years after the coup. Although they have increased slowly, in 1984 they remained at levels far below the precoup period. Within this shrunken budget, the military has been greatly favored. We must conclude that the military has taken away from state spending in other areas. Given the government's general economic philosophy, increases in military spending were possible because of decreases in spending for civil employees (see Tables 20 and 22). In other words, we are saying that given the characteristics of the neoconservative economic model, the growth of military spending did not clash with industrial entrepreneurial activity or with state-fueled industrialization, as in previous decades (see Table 23).

The foregoing helps explain how the armed forces' historical industrializing orientation has been converted into support for a free trade model. The armed forces have maintained their capitalist and authoritarian orientation, but are now more directly at the service of national and international financiers. The social base of support for this program of authoritarian capitalism is much narrower than the support given to the industrialization project. Consequently, the armed forces are much more apt to oppose or repress the Chilean people than cooperate with them.

The benefits conferred on the armed forces by the system may be observed in the statistical synthesis offered in Table 21. When we realize that Table 22 excludes information about the Police Corps and the Bureau of Investigations, and that the source of the information is the U.S. Arms Control and Disarmament Agency, which generally underestimates figures for Latin American countries, it is clear that the place of the armed forces in Chilean society has changed appreciably.

Increased funding for the armed forces has allowed higher wages and salaries. People previously uninterested in a military career have been attracted by the new political role of the armed forces. The quality of enlisted soldiers and officers has thus been enhanced. Modernization and professionalization has meant a greater institutional commitment

TABLE 21
Distribution of Military Expenditures in Chile, 1973-1979 (thousands 1979 US$)

	1973	1974	1975	1976	1977	1978	1979
Police (Carabineros)	97,198.40	148,515.4	122,289.52	126,120.18	159,584.12	180,664.92	199,244.61
Bureau of Investigation	9,964.666	13,871.52	13,299.16	18,185.083	23,219.75	28,803.7	34,209.94
Dept. of War	158,183.36	250,671.93	170,581.49	174,175.16	233,893.73	274,564.55	297,675.0
Dept. of Navy	202,142.8	255,468.61	173,445.78	182,077.7	207,912.16	234,082.36	268,738.18
Dept. of Air Force	97,937.09	85,025.53	115,857.15	75,722.097	107,798.15	126,012.01	147,089.78
Subtotal[a]	565,426.31	753,552.99	595,473.1	576,280.21	732,407.91	844,127.54	946,060.97
General Recruiting Service	770.603	257.0926	259.1911	142.2518	162.2083	261.9297	1,316.3758
Hidographic Institute of the Navy	708.1735	415.6322	275.3154	864.9272	672.8596	1,480.9832	1,415.5503
Air Photogrammetic Service of the Air Force	243.1009	414.2040	229.5791	312.5885	498.0644	684.0410	883.8708
Geographic Institute of the Army	1,734.1138	434.3450	580.225	820.425	1,768.4381	4,936.8662	6,169.7449
FAMAE	10,303.574	12,719.739	11,388.035	23,320.196	26,846.191	22,671.418	17,425.422
ASMAR	17,105.139	20,346.486	20,400.564	15,875.971	19,666.841	29,126.065	34,042.953
Total 1[a]	596,281.99	788,137.48	628,605.98	617,595.54	781,783.22	903,288.88	1,013,081.5
Social Security	172,258.33	261,520.43	202,645.46	208,847.72	285,151.67	295,822.09	n.a.
Nuclear Programme	1,504.5687	2,380.2464	4,013.0268	6,971.9581	10,016.724	11,596.057	14,450.053
Foreign Military Aid	6,710.5044	4,888.2435	3,084.1923	1,671.7872	587.8865	n.a.	n.a.
Total 2[a]	776,755.39	1,056,926.3	841,432.8	835,086.99	1,077,539.3	1,210,706.9	1,323,353.59

[a]Personnel expenditure has been deflated using the wage-and-salaries index of the public sector. Total expenditure was deflated by the consumer price index. Hence, total expenditure figures differ from the sum of their components.

Source: Carlos Portales and Augusto Varas, "The Role of Military Expenditure in the Development Process. Chile 1952-1973 and 1973-1980: Two Contrasting Cases," Ibero-Americana, Nordic Journal of Latin American Studies 12, no. 1-2 (1983):40.

TABLE 22
Ratio of Military Personnel to Civilian Population in Chile, 1971-1980

Year	Armed Forces[a]	Ratio to Population (per thous.)	Teachers/ Military (per thous.)	Physicians/ Military (per thous.)
1971	70,000	7.4	110.0	6.4
1972	75,000	7.7	n.a.	6.0
1973	75,000	7.6	n.a.	7.5
1974	90,000	9.0	132.2	4.8
1975	110,000	10.8	111.8	3.6
1976	111,000	10.7	105.4	4.3
1977	111,000	10.6	113.5	5.9
1978	111,000	10.4	81.0	5.9
1979	111,000	10.3	75.6	5.9
1980	115,000	10.5	72.1	5.9

[a]Figure excludes the National Police (Carabineros) and the Bureau of Investigation.

Sources: 1971-1977: U.S. Arms Control and Disarmament Agency, World Military Expenditures and Arms Transfers 1971-1980 (Washington, D.C.: ACDA, 1983); 1978-1980: Ruth Leger Sivard, World Military and Social Expenditures 1981, 1982, 1983, copyright World Priorities, Washington, D.C. 20007, U.S.A. Used by permission.

TABLE 23
Military Expenditures (Milex) and Gross Geographic Investment (GGI) in Chile, 1973-1979 (1973=100)

	1973	1974	1975	1976	1977	1978	1979
Milex	100	138.0	108.3	107.5	138.7	158.8	170.3
GGI	100	133.8	89.5	86.4	134.8	179.9	219.1

Source: Carlos Portales and Augusto Varas, "The Role of Military Expenditure in the Development Process. Chile 1952-1973 and 1973-1980: Two Contrasting Cases," Ibero-Americana, Nordic Journal of Latin American Studies 12, no. 1-2 (1983):49.

to and internalization of military values. The armed forces have thus come to be identified as a route of social mobility.

This adds up to a new profile for the armed forces within Chilean society and clarifies the features distinguishing them during this period. Their development has revolved around their professional defense activities and their support for the regime, two functions that have been mutually reinforcing.

PROSPECTS FOR CHANGE

The political and economic conditions in this period of military government have made the armed forces the principal support for the regime. Paradoxically, despite what has been analyzed as the monolithic and unconditional support of the armed forces for the government, herein lies their principal weakness.

As the neoconservative economic model was able to deliver direct benefits only to small segments of society (among them the armed forces), the transformation of this period will probably not be institutionalized. The armed forces may continue to provide support as long as the overall political and economic conditions remain unaltered. If alternatives to the mere continuation of the current domination become available, the armed forces will find themselves at a crossroads once again. At that point, the armed forces' noninvolvement in politics and their subordination to executive authority may end, and they will begin a new role in society. The reaffirmation of military professionalism will not suffice when decisions about alternative assignments of state funds will have to be made.

As the armed forces are quite committed to the neoconservative economic model, the recent large-scale crisis will pull the military into the political arena in which economic and social policies are being debated, as in 1974 and 1975. There are many indications that a crisis could be developing as the social and economic effects of the current recession filter through Chilean society.

NOTES

1. This article has been written in a deliberately synthetic fashion. For a more detailed treatment of the topics covered, see Augusto Varas, Felipe Agüero, and Fernando Bustamante, *Chile, democracia y fuerzas armadas* (Santiago: FLACSO, 1980).

2. H. E. Bicheno, "Anti-Parliamentary Themes in Chilean History," *Government and Opposition* 7, no. 3 (Summer 1972).

3. See Augusto Varas and Felipe Aguero, *El projecto político militar* (Santiago: FLACSO, 1984).

4. This process is analyzed in Augusto Varas, "La intervención civil de las fuerzas armadas," in Hugo Frühling, Carlos Portales, and Augusto Varas, *Estado y fuerzas armadas en el proceso político chileno* (Santiago: FLACSO, 1983).

5. Comprehensive studies on the evolution of military spending in Chile can be found in Gertrude E. Heare, *Trends in Latin American Military Expenditures* (Washington, D.C.: U.S. Department of State, December 1971), and in Joseph E. Loftus, *Latin American Defense Expenditures, 1938–1965* (Santa Monica, Calif.: RAND Corporation, 1980).

6. With regard to U.S. pressure on the Chilean armed forces, see two publications by the U.S. Senate Select Committee to Study Governmental Operations with Respect to Intelligence Activities: *Alleged U.S. Involvement in Assassination Plots in Five Foreign Countries* (Washington, D.C.: Government

Printing Office, 1975) and *Covert Action in Chile, 1963–1973* (Washington, D.C.: Government Printing Office, 1975).

7. A study of these relations is found in Genaro Arriagada, "El marco institucional de las fuerzas armadas" (Paper presented to the workshop, Six Years of Military Government in Chile, Woodrow Wilson International Center for Scholars, Washington, D.C., 1980).

8. See note 4 above.

9. Demilitarization, Disarmament, and Democracy

The armed forces in Latin America have historically oscillated between supporting industrialization and its benefits to the entrepreneurial sectors and supporting conservative, repressive projects in reaction to worker or leftist political movements. Only marginally, in very few countries and for very limited periods, have the armed forces participated in projects of social transformation, in which the Latin American left and worker or peasant sectors have played a considerable role. This happened in Peru in 1968 and in Panama during the administration of Omar Torrijos, which conducted negotiations with the United States over the Panama Canal.

Nonetheless, the armed forces are not exclusively the armed branch of the bourgeoisie. The historical developments analyzed in preceding chapters indicate that the Latin American armed forces have acquired institutional interests of their own that do not always fully coincide with classist political projects in the region. The armed forces of the continent have attained increasing autonomy relative to local politics and politicians. Thus, the congruence between the diverse alternatives of state organization and military aspirations does not indicate a projection of class interests within military headquarters. Any attempt to stabilize a permanent democratic order in Latin America must take this political reality into account.

A new type of civil-military relationship structured according to the values and criteria of democracy must have as its principal objective the reduction of the present level of military autonomy. The redefinition of civil-military relations will require an analysis of the principal motives of the armed forces to perform a salient political role in the region.[1] The military in Latin America has absorbed conservative ideological influences both from conservative sectors of their own society and from corresponding external forces. The armed forces have further developed and incorporated conservative perspectives regarding their own organization. Finally, the armed forces have been free of the civilian control that could neutralize them politically and convert them into supporters of democratic regimes.

These three aspects of the history of the military in Latin America explain the conflictive and unstable character of civil-military relations and suggest, at the same time, the direction that change must adopt. In order to redefine the relationship between the citizenry and the armed forces, the military's ideological universe must be reframed, their international ties shifted, their method of internal organization altered, and their ties with the rest of the state restructured. Only then can the armed forces be fully integrated into a democratic order.

All sectors of society will have to participate in this transformation of the military, in order to redefine its objectives, adjust its means, and coordinate it with the rest of state and society. This participation will ensure a truly democratic nature for the new civil-military relations, and ensure their stability and efficiency. It will also help to overcome the historical absence of civilian political and institutional administration of the armed forces.

A new position for the armed forces in regional life entails not only the redefinition of the military's institutional connection with the state and society as a whole, but also a refiguring of civilian participation in military activities. The participation of military personnel in national democratic life and the participation of civilians in military activities must be significantly altered. The normalization of democracy requires the application of constitutional principles to the military institution and its obedience to legitimately generated and exercised civilian power. Thus the armed forces will be restored to the discharge of their proper function, the defense of the sovereignty and territorial integrity of the nation.

This approach to the process of institutional redefinition is supported, moreover, by the coherence that social mobilization through democracy must have. The growing participation of a stable majority forms the foundation of a democratic regime, in which decision-making is one of the principal aspects of social political life. The ideological content of this process is expressed in the popular demand for the recuperation and development of democratic rights, and in the claims of democratic theories that forbid the participation of purely functional institutions, such as the military, in politics.

The return of the armed forces to their proper professional function is the principal element of a return to democracy. The basic problems of institutional development and the scope and nature of military participation in the formulation of national defense policy can be defined from this perspective. The main responsibility of civilian forces is to determine a national defense policy that would be consonant with the national project of democratic development. This would include determining the goals and means of national defense and the role of the military in this project, all within the context of democracy.

A policy oriented toward avoiding military segregation and stimulating the integration of the citizenry must ensure some civilian participation in military affairs, relate national defense institutions to other state structures, and incorporate the military into national democratic life. These factors constitute the pillars of the democratization of the armed forces.

PARTICIPATION IN MILITARY AFFAIRS
AND INSTITUTIONAL RELATIONS

The first aspect to be considered is the civilian direction of military policy. The national defense forces depend upon executive power as it is exercised through the national defense ministry. In a democracy, national defense policy must be conceived and elaborated by pluralist and collective organisms. This is designated by law and political constitutions, without weakening the representation and incorporation of civilians. In these collective organisms or national defense councils, participants include those with government responsibilities over foreign relations, economic development, communications and transportation, and national defense, as well as members of principal civilian groups and organizations. The military high command should counsel the executive in the formulation of defense policy, and develop it through the defense ministry.

In this way, the democratic principle of the subordination of military institutions to civilian power will be shaped. A basic task for civilians will be to formulate a defense policy that coordinates military activity with national development as a whole. This will entail civilian stewardship of the military. As an example, the defense minister will have to be evaluated with regard to his ability to conduct defense policy, and not, as has occurred in the majority of Latin American countries, with respect to his ability to represent and express the corporatism of the military institutions. Parliament, as a representative institution that expresses the general will of the people, must also take an active part in the formation of military policy and the life of military institutions. Beyond its legislative functions, parliament must regularly evaluate the functioning and situation of the armed forces.

The armed forces will interact with other branches of the state only as a consultant, and exclusively for the definition of policies related to their institutions. There must not be, therefore, a military presence in organizations or institutions that define typically civilian policies. In this way, the military's tendency to interfere in the definition of all state policies will be deactivated. The proper function of the military is to defend the territorial integrity of a nation against possible foreign aggression, and because foreign policy is one of the principal instruments of defense policy, the armed forces must be constantly briefed on the progress of foreign relations. This process will be institutionalized through national defense councils.

Foreign relations are often contained within more or less formalized military ties between nations. Reciprocally, military ties are often constrained or determined by the diplomatic relations between countries. In a stable democracy, international military ties of the armed forces must be directed and coordinated by state foreign policy. This will require the close collaboration of the foreign relations and national defense ministers.

The activities of the armed forces are also related, directly or indirectly, to schemes of production and development. It therefore falls upon the armed forces to participate in the definition of these activities, although their management need not necessarily remain in military hands. At the least, these activities must be coordinated with other pertinent public organisms, to take advantage of their resources.

The armed forces are also involved in and affected by other state economic activities (housing, economy, planning) inasmuch as they require public financing. The military is further responsible for advising and coordinating state expenditures for military acquisitions, transportation, energy, and public infrastructure. This advisory and coordinating role within other public organisms will be implemented through national defense ministries and institutionalized via national defense councils that prevent the political weight of the armed forces from exceeding that of other state organs.

In the area of military education, the armed forces will become thoroughly involved in schools, academies, and institutes. In order to close the gap between the military and the rest of society, this involvement must not be seen as contrary to the orientations and regulations of the national educational system of a democratic society. These will be formulated and implemented by the ministries of education for the entire society. The military educational activity, however, must be related and coordinated to civilian activity in this area, and be subject as well to common evaluations, guidelines, and curriculum requirements. This will be achieved through a variety of measures: equivalencies between military and civilian titles and degrees of different levels must be determined; procedures and prerequisites for entrance into civilian and military educational institutes must be standardized; the exchange of professors and courses between the two types of establishments, particularly at the university level, must be facilitated; joint programs to improve university courses must be developed; teaching plans and curricular guidelines must be formulated within the ministries of education (except for strictly military areas of instruction, which the national defense council will oversee); the same bodies that regulate civilian educational institutes must evaluate and direct the general curricula of military institutes; these bodies must further investigate and supervise study abroad; and the armed forces and other public institutions involved in higher education must cooperate in the area of scientific and technological research.

PARTICIPATION OF MEMBERS OF THE ARMED FORCES IN NATIONAL DEMOCRATIC LIFE

The insertion of military *institutions* into national democratic life must be complemented by the full participation of particular *members* of the armed forces in civilian life. The armed forces, by virtue of their responsibility for the defense of national territory, must not participate in specifically civilian institutions. However, as members of society and as citizens, they must share civilian rights and duties. In this way, the essential democratic rights of all people will be recognized. Further, basic conditions for an active relationship between distinct national groups and sectors and the military will be established, facilitating the consolidation of democracy in the state and society.

A constitutive aspect of a democratic society is the right of its members to participate in public administration. This principle should be realized for all military personnel—officers, noncommissioned officers, and enlisted soldiers—through universal secret vote in free and periodic elections. Although the mere fact of being members of society is reason enough for the right to vote, their function in the defense of the homeland and their absolute institutional subordination to the power emanating from the people underscores their full access to this right, and further obliges them to be completely and directly informed on all issues submitted to a vote. Fair regulation of the participation of military personnel in elections will eliminate confusion over their function in this regard. However, military personnel should not run for public office while they remain in military institutions.

The rights to freedom of thought, conscience, and religion must be upheld within military quarters in the freedom to think and adhere to the orders presented to them. These rights must not be limited by any coercion or pressure, whether physical, psychological, or moral. The civilian equivalent of these freedoms consists of the right to publicly manifest any belief, thought, or religion. Intimately linked to this are the rights of freedom of research, opinion, expression, and diffusion— the right to externalize thoughts or opinions through any means. There is also the right to learn about other opinions, ideas, thoughts, and information. Any form of prior censorship is inadmissible.

Restrictions on these freedoms must apply to everyone equally, without apologias on the exigencies of "security," or any other euphemisms used to disguise discrimination, hostility, or violence. Rights must be protected, particularly among members of the military, through ready access to the variety of printed materials that circulate among the public. Further, both the military and the citizenry have the right to freedom of association. They should be able to participate in peaceful meetings with other persons in order to promote ideas of a religious, political, social, or recreational nature. Here we would underscore that the military function, inasmuch as it is a part of the overall state function, obligates the members of the armed forces to hold political ideas that are in harmony with the functioning of a democratic society. The principle of nondeliberation within the framework of formal constitutionalism has not historically prevented a degree of discriminate deliberation within the military hierarchy. At lower levels of the military hierarchy, the free circulation of ideas was inhibited. This restriction on the free movement of ideas and thought has impaired the institutionalization and expansion of democracy. To formalize and generalize the democratic rights to members of the military does not, then, do more than recognize a reality: as persons and free citizens, they share these rights. The actual practice of these rights by military personnel will not impede their normal functioning or the effectiveness of their mission.

Cultural rights must also be preserved. The arts and intellectual life must be promoted for the enjoyment of all. Cultural life must reach military quarters as well—to expand their world view and encompass nonmilitary aspects of life. The socioeconomic rights that should prevail for the majority of the population are basically the rights to an adequate standard of living and social security. Guarantees of health and well-being, social services, and continual improvement of the standard of living must not discriminate between civilians and members of the military. Society must effectively safeguard the economic and social rights of uniformed personnel according to norms that apply to all citizens.

Labor rights that guarantee dignity in the workplace must be adequately protected by impartial legislation. These rights should be extended to the military and should include, in times of peace, the right of military personnel to relax and the limitation of their working hours. Rights of equal opportunity should be protected regarding promotion to higher rank, and information concerning the mechanisms and criteria for promotions and assignments should be readily available. In the area of civil rights, military personnel should have the freedom to marry and raise families. In many countries of Latin America this is now subject to the approval of a higher authority. Finally, the right of military personnel to form unions must be recognized. These unions should be protected by mechanisms distinct from those governing civilian unions. These measures will renovate military institutions and expand their cultural life.

In almost all Latin American countries military service is fulfilled through a draft system. The restrictions on individual freedom and on the freedom to work that the fulfillment of this duty entails must be regulated by determining a fixed duration of service. This will facilitate the reentry of an individual into civilian life following military duty. Within institutional necessities, this will grant a certain margin for requesting the place of assignment. An elementary democratic right of citizens is the right to decline military duty on the grounds of conscientious objection. An alternative military service oriented toward the benefit of the community should be provided. This will further enable the fulfillment of duty, whether military or civilian, to be free of sex or age discrimination.

Another basic right of citizens is equality before the law. Within the framework of democratic civil-military relations, the absolute dominion of judicial power over the administration of justice, and the absolute independence of all the courts, including military, with respect to every other political, administrative, or military authority should be guaranteed. Judicial power, by means of professional court associations, must review military court decisions. The operation of military tribunals should be restricted to times of external war declared by the president of the republic and authorized by parliament. Peacetime military trials should be independent of the military hierarchy and their jurisdiction should be limited to military crimes as defined by the code of laws.

MILITARY STRENGTH FOR NATIONAL DEFENSE

Peace, as an objective of the democratic state, should be the goal and purpose of the defense policy. A deterrent military power should be generated and maintained simultaneously with real proposals for arms limitation leading to complete and total disarmament. Defense policies in Latin America should be oriented toward deterring potential aggressors, avoiding situations that could become scenes of international conflict, and maintaining a position of nonalignment in foreign policy. National war capability should neither be considered nor developed with regard to an eventual nuclear holocaust instigated by the superpowers.

The arms race of the last decade in Latin America has given the nations of the continent increasing access to sophisticated weaponry that often far surpasses their actual defense needs. The plethora of weapons systems provided by diverse suppliers reflects the success of supplier companies more than it does the particular needs of each country.

In contrast to this pattern, a democratic national defense strategy would require coordinating military development with the objectives of the democratic state. This coordination should address the maintenance of highly efficient armed forces for defense purposes, designed for deterrence. The maintenance of a deterrent power of extreme effectiveness requires some deployment of modern, technologically advanced mobile weaponry. Thus, the development of the military must be oriented toward qualitative rather than quantitative achievements. A modern and effective military system that is small but has ample capacity to deter potential aggressors should be designed.

Defensive weapons systems and strategies should be the focus of the Latin American military. Because attack can be an element of defense, some weapons must serve both purposes. However, a general design based on defense would grant the fundamental criteria for discriminating among different types of weapons. In this sense, it is evident, for example, that strategic range missiles, bombers, and aircraft carriers are beyond strictly defensive necessities. Distinct systems should be put together according to the type of material required for air, land, or sea war. This perspective conforms completely, furthermore, with the objectives of economic development, not only because their objectives are in harmony, but also because defensive weapons systems would be available at a comparatively low cost. The military would not be draining funds needed for development.

In financing the armed forces, it should be recognized that armed institutions have already achieved a level of modernization greatly superior to the historical average. This process has delayed improvements in the standard of living for broad social sectors. It is necessary, therefore, to limit the resources allocated to the national defense effort. This limit on military expenditures should be related to the institutional development strategy. The development of deterrent power in a context of arms limitations at a regional or subregional level can be maximized through the renovation of existing material.

Increasing costs of national defense are evidently the result of the size of the contingent in active service. For this reason, an institutional policy of reducing troop size without weakening deterrent capability would not only maintain and increase levels of modernization, but would also reduce global expenditures in this area. Such a project would require an in-depth review of the situation of regular and complementary personnel and their effective adaptation to deterrent capability.

Decisions on military expenditures should be made together with decisions on social expenditures for health, education, housing, and so on. As a general criterion, military expenditures should not surpass state expenditures in any of these areas. Only increases in both areas would permit the expansion of military expenditures without prejudicing the population.

EXTERNAL INITIATIVES FOR NATIONAL DEFENSE AND PEACE

National defense policies must be coordinated with foreign policies in pursuing initiatives on arms limitation and eventual total disarmament. A policy of peace and friendship, coupled with broad and diversified alliances in the international sphere, constitutes the most solid guarantee of national security. The maintenance of relations with all the countries of the world and broad participation in the international scene could promote cooperation, integrity, and self-determination of all peoples.

Because foreign policy expresses national interests as they are democratically determined by the people, it is necessarily independent. The development of an independent foreign policy does not contradict international agreements nor the promotion of accords and multilateral obligations, inasmuch as they comply with the free initiative of the country and conform with its interests. However, history teaches that an independent policy must be separated from adhesion to any blocs that would subordinate national interests to those of the hegemonic power in the area. An effective strategy of nonalignment is complementary to an independent policy.

Latin America needs an independent international initiative. The aspects of subordination contained within the Interamerican Reciprocal Assistance Treaty and subsequently manifested in several events in the region should be specifically approached and overcome. The conception embodied in this treaty—that the Latin American countries should be integrated into a U.S.-led military bloc—is obsolete in Latin America. The majority of countries in the region have experienced the negative aspects of this treaty—for example, during the Malvinas conflict.

One of the principal responsibilities of the foreign policy of democratic states in Latin America is to make regional initiatives in favor of peace. These initiatives express, on the international plane, the defensive orientation of the military institution and its weapons system. In effect, a national defense policy oriented toward creating a deterrent power must be complemented by an equally defensive structuring of the military capability of all countries of the region. Broadcasting and institutionalizing this conception is a specific aspect of a foreign policy of peace on the continent. It will be realized through a variety of multilateral measures designed to put an end to the arms race and to restrict military might to the exact defensive needs of each country.

The increased contention between the United States and the Soviet Union has colored and pervaded the entire international system during recent years, despite important pressure for détente. This predominance of conflictive East-West dynamics has limited the opportunity for a reorganization of the international order that would address the problems of the South. Moreover, in the exclusively bipolar and reductionist logic of these dynamics, tensions within the Third World have been interpreted as a by-product or manifestation of East-West conflict, denying local realities, conflicts, and forces.

Inter-American relations have consistently expressed a national security doctrine that sees all forces promoting structural change as agents of the opposing bloc or as the vanguard of an extracontinental military threat. The perspective that prevails within the U.S. government unfortunately parallels that maintained by the Latin American armed forces in recent decades—just as many of these armed forces are vacating governments in favor of civilian rule.

A new democratic foreign policy will strengthen the independence and autonomy of Latin America so as to promote its political, social, and economic development in the international context. To achieve this, the region must be extricated from the dynamics of global conflicts. With this in mind, the content of "national security" should be reformulated to separate the choice of political regime and national development projects from the security concerns that are imposed on the region. The nexus established within the national security doctrine between East-West conflict and the dynamics of regional domestic politics must be broken.

It is necessary, consequently, to guarantee that Latin America actually be a peace zone,[2] to which there can be no internal or external military threat. This new approach should reestablish the distinction between external security and internal order. This implies, on the one hand, the acceptance by the United States of a notion of continental security centered on the avoidance of military threat and on the sociopolitical nature of Latin American regimes. On the other hand, it implies the reprofessionalization of the armed forces toward external defense, leaving the tasks of policy and internal order to other institutions.

The creation of a peace zone should also include guarantees against military aggression from within the region and against external intervention into Latin America. The peace zone should be oriented toward achieving complete denuclearization of Latin America, eliminating all bases or other military presence of foreign powers in the zone, limiting and reducing arms in the region, and promoting the superpowers' acceptance of this new regional statute. The zone should be based upon a Latin American nonaggression pact and on the strengthening of political mechanisms and negotiation as a way of overcoming intraregional conflicts. Old disputes and territorial demands within Latin America must be resolved completely through law and regional integration. This is not a utopian proposal; consider, for example, the cooperation in recent decades between countries as previously hostile as France and Germany. The peace zone must be made a priority of democratic foreign policy, to be promoted through increasingly inclusive bilateral and multilateral initiatives. A new security policy that excludes Latin America as a war threat zone should open the region to a wide range of possible international ties.

Regional disengagement from global conflict and East-West tensions will not mean disengagement from international relations. To the contrary, Latin America will be able to play a greater role, perhaps as an arbiter, in favor of détente and peaceful international negotiation to resolve these disputes. The region could also contribute consistent policies against colonialism, racism, militarism, and other dangerous or hostile tendencies in the world. Active participation in the nonaligned movement, in which Latin American countries are being steadily and significantly incorporated, will strengthen the most important forums for international political action for countries of the Third World.

PEACE MOVEMENTS AND DEMOCRACY

No quantity of measures to disarm and demilitarize the region will be successful without popular support and commitment. This support must come fundamentally from civil society, mobilized through nongovernmental organizations.

The crisis of Latin American states has revealed a growing contradiction between the true needs of the nations and the particular requirements of different state institutions. As long as the military continues to define and promote its own institutional needs and goals above those of society, clashes and contradiction will occur. Changing this situation is central to controlling and diminishing the arms race.

The lack of a national democratic rule renders the state unable to control its member institutions or to allocate resources according to society's real needs. Within the arms race, for example, the state is unable to control the military, stop the arms buildup, or ratify and implement disarmament agreements according to the general desire for peace. Military governments—regardless of their class orientation[3]—come to embody only their own corporate autonomy and to impose their own institutional projects on society. This intensifies the contradictions between the state—in this case under military control—and the rest of society.

This crisis of the state, which results from the lack of popular participation, determines the state's behavior on the international level, especially regarding disarmament. As long as disarmament proposals and agreements are formulated and implemented through intergovernmental consultations or international organizations, only imbalanced relations are possible among these states. A state in crisis lacks the relative power necessary to push through a proposal or to fulfill and enforce the international agreements it has endorsed. This is true not only for military, but for financial, economic, and political agreements as well.[4] It is thus unrealistic to expect balanced, stable, and trustworthy international relations from a state in crisis. This problem becomes especially serious in the case of Latin American military governments—an exceptional and paradoxical case of state crisis—for whom disarmament and arms limitation agreements could result in institutional suicide.

The implementation of actual disarmament and arms limitation measures has thus been relatively ineffective. Most of these proposals are state oriented, in accordance with the state-to-state links characteristic of international relations. The primary structural obstacle to disarmament and arms limitation efforts is the current state impotence to control military expenditures or enforce arms limitation. The role of international intergovernmental bodies in pursuing multilateral arms limitation and disarmament agreements is paramount, particularly for global treaties and comprehensive disarmament strategies. However, to be successful in Latin America, these efforts must be coordinated and complemented with disarmament activities originating from the people to stop the regional arms race as well.

This perspective was stressed at the United Nations by the Expert-Consultant Group, which called for the participation of the population of all countries in a more active, coherent, and organized manner than we see today. Different movements and organizations of political, professional, or religious nature can play an important role in this respect, as they have effectively in the past. Negative consequences of the arms race are affecting all peoples of the world, threatening their existence, and impose great social and economic pains. The people of the world have a self-evident right to receive information on military government policies and programs and on their consequences.[5]

Unfortunately, the Expert-Consultant Group has not yet followed up on its recommendations, which are especially relevant in their acknowledgment of the problems caused by the arms race to national programs of development. From the author's point of view, the group's recommendations are of utmost significance.

Latin American states have to be democratized in order to secure the enforcement of intergovernmental agreements. This will require structural changes that, in the long run, will include channels for the participation of the people. The arms race, however, cannot wait. Its negative effects must be stopped urgently and globally. The enforcement of disarmament and arms limitation agreements should also be the concern of people organized in current international and local nongovernmental organizations and in a network for regional disarmament.

According to our analysis, Latin American efforts regarding arms limitation and disarmament have failed because of the inability of Latin American governments to control their own military institutions.[6] Military governments are a dramatic consequence of this problem. New civil-military relations must therefore be created, together with new and different approaches to arms limitation and disarmament. State-oriented policies have proved ineffective. Nevertheless, they ought to be maintained, developed, and coordinated with nongovernmental efforts. Greater emphasis should be put on nongovernmental peace research and action-oriented organizations, both on a regional and national scale, underlining the relevance of a close link between these efforts and those of international organizations devoted to peace. Special efforts to create both stable peace research and action-oriented organizations and to provide the public with information about peace problems through regular educational programs and publication in the mass media should be made.[7]

All the proposals formulated herein, plus many others that are being generated within our militarized societies, are oriented toward combining the democratization of Latin American societies with the socialization of military power. This dual process will include the deconcentration and decentralization of decision-making on national defense matters, and the social affirmation of the grand ideal of all people living together in peace.

NOTES

1. My analysis follows the work of the Subcommittee on Armed Forces of the Grupo de Estudios Constitucionales (or the "Group of 24") organized by the Chilean democratic forces, of which I was a member. A more developed framework of this same proposal can be found in Augusto Varas, Felipe Agüero, and Fernando Bustamante, *Chile, democracia y fuerzas armadas* (Santiago, Chile: FLACSO, 1980).

2. The ideas on the peace zone presented here were originally set forth in Gustavo Lagos, Heraldo Muñoz, Carlos Portales, and Augusto Varas, *Democracia y política exterior: Una propuesta para la recuperación de las relaciones internacionales de Chile* (Santiago: ACHIP, May 1983).

3. Military governments, whether "fascist" or not, always express class interests. The realization of class interest by the military results in an even greater autonomy of the military within the state structure.

4. Chile, for instance, has ratified the "International Covenant on Civil and Political Rights" but has never enforced it, arguing that there were procedural obstacles.

5. United Nations, *Las consecuencias económicas y sociales de la carrera de armamentos y de los gastos militares* (New York: United Nations, 1972, 1978), pp. 84–85.

6. Raimo Väyrynen, "Restraints of the International Transfer of Arms and Military Technology," *Alternatives* 3 (1978).

7. See Malvern Lumsden, "Militarism: Cultural Dimensions of Militarization" (Paper presented at the Pugwash Symposium on Militarism, Oslo, November 1977).

Acronyms

ACDA	Arms Control and Disarmament Agency (United States)
ACHIP	Asociacion Chilena de Investigaciones para la Paz; Chilean Peace Research Association
APSI	Agencia Periodistica y Servicios Informativos
CED	Centro de Estudios del Desarrollo (Chile)
CEDES	Centro de Estudios Economicos y Sociales (Argentina)
CIDE	Centro de Investigacion y Docencia en Economia (Mexico)
CIEPLAN	Corporacion de Investigaciones Economicas para America Latina (Chile)
CISEC	Centro de Investigaciones Socioeconomicas (Chile)
COIN	counterinsurgency
COPEI	Christian Democratic Party of Venezuela
DGFM	Direccion General de Fabricaciones Militares; General Directorate for Ordnance Production
DoD	Department of Defense (United States)
EMBRAER	Empresa Brasileira de Aeronautica; Brazilian Aeronautics Company
ENGESA	Empresa Especializada de Ingenieria (Brazil)
ERP	Ejercito Revolucionario de Pueblo; People's Revolutionary Army (Argentina)
FARC	Revolutionary Armed Forces of Colombia
FLACSO	Latin American Faculty of Social Sciences
FMS	foreign military sales
GNP	gross national product
IDS	Institute for Development Studies (Great Britain)
IMBEL	Industria de Material Belico de Brazil; War Material Industry of Brazil

IMET	International Military Education and Training
NOVIB	Netherlands Organization for International Cooperation and Development
OAS	Organization of American States
OPEC	Organization of Petroleum-Exporting Countries
R&D	research and development
SAIS	School of Advanced International Studies (United States)
SAM	surface-to-air missile
SAREC	Swedish Agency for Research Cooperation with Developing Countries
SELA	Latin American Economic System
SIPRI	Stockholm International Peace Research Institute
UNESCO	United Nations Educational, Scientific, and Cultural Organization

Selected Bibliography

Abdel-Malek, Anouar. *La dialéctica social.* Mexico City: Siglo XXI, 1975.

Albrecht, Ulrich. "The Cost of Armamentism." *Journal of Peace Research,* no. 3 (1973).

———. "Armament and Inflation." *Instant Research on Peace and Violence* (Tampere, Finland), no. 3 (1974).

———. "Arms Trade with the Third World and Domestic Arms Production." *Instant Research on Peace and Violence* (Tampere, Finland), no. 1-2 (1976).

Althaus, Peter. "La evolución de la doctrina militar norteamericana después de 1945." *Memorial del Ejército de Chile,* no. 356 (July-August 1970).

Amaral Jurgel, José Alfredo. *Segurança e democracia.* Rio de Janeiro: Livraria Jose Olimpo Editora, 1975.

Arriagada, Genaro. "El marco institucional de las fuerzas armadas." Paper presented to the workshop, Six Years of Military Government in Chile, Woodrow Wilson International Center for Scholars, Washington, D.C., 1980.

Arriazu, Ricardo H. "Movimientos internacionales de capitales." *Cuadernos de la CEPAL,* no. 32 (1979).

Asociación Chilena de Investigaciones para la Paz (ACHIP). *Democracia y política exterior: Una propuesta para la recuperación de las relaciones internacionales de Chile.* Santiago: ACHIP, May 1983.

Atkins, G. Pope. *Arms and Politics in the Dominican Republic.* Boulder, Colo.: Westview Press, 1981.

Baño, Rodrigo. "El conflicto político en América Latina." *Documento de Trabajo.* FLACSO, Santiago, 1977.

Barros, Alexandre S. C. "The Diplomacy of National Security: South American International Relations in a Defrosting World." In Roland G. Hellman and H. Jon Rosenbaum, eds., *Latin America: The Search for a New International Role.* New York: Sage Publications, 1975.

———. "The Formulation and Orientation of Brazilian Diplomacy." Paper presented at the seminar, Comparative Latin American Foreign Policies, Viña del Mar, Chile, September 20–23, 1982.

Bauffre, Andre. *Estrategia para la acción.* Buenos Aires: Ediciones Pleamar, 1975.

Bettelheim, Charles. "Remarques theoriques." In Arghiri Emmanuel, *L'Echange inegal.* Paris: Maspero, 1969.

Bicheno, H. E. "Anti-Parliamentary Themes in Chilean History." *Government and Opposition* 7, no. 3 (Summer 1972).

Black, Jan K. "The Military and Political Decompression in Brazil." *Armed Forces and Society,* Summer 1980.

Bobrow, Davis. "The Civic Role of the Military." *Western Political Quarterly*, March 1922.

Boils, Guillermo. "Tendencias reformistas de los militares latinoamericanos en el período entre guerras." National University of Mexico, Mexico, 1977. Typescript.

Booth, David, and Bernardo Sorj. *Military Reformism and Social Classes: The Peruvian Experience*. New York: St. Martin's Press, 1983.

Boudon, Raymond. *La logique du social*. Paris: Hachette, 1979.

Bradford, Zeb B., and Frederick J. Brown. "Apoyo del ejercito a la coalición de seguridad." *Military Review*, May 1972.

Brigagao, Clovis. "The Case of Brazil: Fortress or Paper Curtain?" *Impact* 31, no. 1 (January-March 1981).

———. *A corrida para a morte: Desarme o mundo armado*. Rio de Janeiro: Editora Nueva Fronteira, 1983.

———. *O mercado de seguranca*. Rio de Janeiro: Editora Nova Fronteira, 1984.

Brogan, Christopher. "Military Higher Education and the Emergence of New Professionalism: Some Consequences for Civil-Military Relations in Latin America." *Army Review*, January 1982.

Buhrer, Jean-Claude. "De multiples conflicts troublent les relations entre nations latino-americanines." *Le Monde*, February 21, 1979.

Burton, James W. *System, State Diplomacy and Rules*. New York: Cambridge University Press, 1968.

Cahn, Anne Hessing, and Joseph J. Kruzel. "Arms Trade in the 1980's." In A. H. Cahn, J. J. Kruzel, P. M. Dawkins, and Jacques Huntzinger, *Controlling Future Arms Trade*. New York: McGraw-Hill for the Council on Foreign Relations, 1977.

Carranza, Mario E. "The Role of Military Expenditure in the Development Process: The Argentinian Case 1946–1980." *Nordic Journal of Latin American Studies*, no. 1-2 (1983).

Case, Robert P. "El entrenamiento de militares latinoamericanos en los Estados Unidos." *Aportes*, October 1976.

Chateau, Jorge. "Características principales del pensamiento geopolítico chileno: Análisis de dos libros." *Documento de Trabajo*. FLACSO, Santiago, 1977.

Chenery, Hollis, et al. *Redistribution with Growth*. Oxford: Oxford University Press for the World Bank and IDS, 1974.

Child, John. "Geopolitical Thinking in Latin America." *Latin American Research Review* 14, no. 2 (1979).

———. *Unequal Alliance: The Inter-American Military System, 1938–1978*. Boulder, Colo.: Westview Press, 1980.

Comblin, Jose. *The Church and the National Security States*. Maryknoll, N.Y.: Orbis Books, 1979.

Corbett, Charles. "The Latin American Military as a Socio-Political Force: Case Studies of Bolivia and Argentina." Center for Advanced Studies, University of Miami, Florida, 1972.

Cordero, Fernando. "Comercio exterior e industria de armas livianas en Argentina, Colombia, Costa Rica, Chile, República Dominicana, Perú, México y Venezuela." *Nordic Journal of Latin American Studies*, no. 1-2 (1983).

Costa Pinto, Luis. "Sociología del nuevo militarismo." *Panorama Económico*, December 1969.

Cuellar, Oscar. "Notas sobre la participación política de los militares en América Latina." *Aportes*, January 1971.

De Andrade, O. "Nuevas formas de hegemonía militar en América Latina." *Canadian Journal of Latin American Studies* 3, nos. 5 and 6 (1978).

De Vries, Barend A. "Public Policy and the Private Sector." In *Finance and Development*. Washington, D.C.: IMF and World Bank, 1981.

Dowse, Robert E. "The Military and Political Development." In Colin Leys, ed., *Politics and Change in Developing Countries*. Cambridge: Cambridge University Press, 1969.

Echeverría, José Medina. "América Latina en los escenarios posibles de la distensión." *Revista de la CEPAL*, 1976.

Einaudi, Luigi, H. Heymann, Jr., D. Ronfeldt, and C. Sereseres. "Transferencia de armas a Latinoamérica: Hacia una política de respeto mutuo." In CIDE, *La dependencia militar latinoamericana*. Mexico City: CIDE, 1978.

Ejército del Ecuador. "El ejército en el desarrollo nacional." *Ejército Nacional* (Quito, Ecuador), February 1976.

"EMBRAER: Alas del Brasil." *Defensa*, no. 21 (January 1980).

Encinas del Pando, José A. "The Role of Military Expenditures in the Development Process, Peru: A Case Study, 1950–1980." *Nordic Journal of Latin American Studies*, no. 1-2 (1983).

Ficht, John S. "The Political Impact of U.S. Military Aid to Latin America: Institutional and Individual Effects." *Armed Forces and Society*, Spring 1979.

Finer, Samuel. *Los militares en la política mundial*. Buenos Aires: Editora Sudamericana, 1969.

Fossum, Egil. "Factors Influencing the Occurrence of Military Coup d'Etat in Latin America." *Journal of Peace Research* (Oslo), no. 3 (1967).

Foxley, Alejandro. *Latin American Experiments in Neo-Conservative Economics*. Berkeley: University of California Press, 1983.

Frenkel, Roberto. "El desarrollo reciente de mercado de capitales en la Argentina." *Desarrollo Económico*, no. 78 (July-September 1980).

Furtado, Celso. "De la ideología del progreso a la ideología del desarrollo." *Universidad de las Naciones Unidas*, HSDRSCA-725/UNUP-298, 1981.

Gallegos, E. "Triunfo en Perú: Un estudio de la contrainsurgencia." *Military Review*, February 1966.

Garretón, Manuel Antonio. "De la seguridad nacional a la nueva institucionalidad." *Foro Internacional*, July-September 1978.

George, Alan L., D. K. Hall, and W. E. Simons. *The Limits of Coercive Diplomacy*. Boston: Little, Brown, 1974.

George, Alan L., and R. Smoke. *Deterrence in American Foreign Policy*. New York: Columbia University Press, 1971.

Gorostiaga, Xabier. *Los banqueros del imperio*. Costa Rica: EDUCA, 1979.

Gramsci, Antonio. *Oeuvres choisies*. Paris: Editions Sociales, 1959.

Grimmett, Richard F. "Trends in Conventional Arms Transfers to the Third World by Major Supplier, 1976–1983." Congressional Research Service, Report no. 84-82 F, May 7, 1984.

Grossman, Claudio. "The U.N. and the OAS: Some Competence Issues in the Peace and Security Field." Ph.D. diss., Utrecht University, 1982.

Guertner, Gary L. "The 74-Day War: New Technology and Old Tactics." *Military Review*, November 1982.

Guglialmelli, E. "Las fuerzas armadas en América Latina: Fuerzas armadas y revolución nacional." *Estrategia* (Argentina), July-August 1972.

Haar, James C. "Ayuda militar para la América Latina." *Military Review*, May 1969.

Halperin, Tulio. *Historia contemporanea de América Latina.* Madrid: Alianza Editorial, 1967.

Hayes, Margaret Daly. "Brazil and the South Atlantic." SAIS, Johns Hopkins University, Washington, D.C., 1981.

Heare, Gertrude E. *Trends in Latin American Military Expenditures.* Washington, D.C.: U.S. Department of State, December 1971.

Hennessy, Alistair. "The Military in Politics." In Claudio Veliz, *Latin America and the Caribbean.* London: Anthony Blond, 1968.

Hirschman, Albert O. "Ideologies of Economic Development in Latin America." In A. O. Hirschman, ed., *Latin American Economic Issues.* New York: Twentieth Century Fund, 1961.

Horowitz, Irving Louis. "Los militares en América Latina." In S. M. Lipset and A. Solari, *Elites y desarrollo en América Latina.* Buenos Aires: Paidos, 1971.

Horowitz, Irving Louis, and Ellen Kay Teinberger. "State Power and Military Nationalism in Latin America." *Comparative Politics,* January 1967.

Hudson, Rexford A. "The Brazilian Way to Technological Independence: Foreign Joint Ventures and the Aircraft Industry." *Inter-American Economic Affairs,* Autumn 1983.

Huntington, Samuel. *The Soldier and the State.* New York: Random House, 1957.

————. *El orden político y las sociedades en cambio.* Buenos Aires: Paidos, 1972.

Huntzinger, Jacques. "Regional Recipients Restraints." In A. H. Cahn, J. J. Kruzel, P. M. Dawkins, and Jacques Huntzinger, *Controlling Future Arms Trade.* New York: McGraw-Hill for the Council on Foreign Relations, 1977.

Hyman, Elizabeth. "Soldiers in Politics: New Insights on Latin American Armed Forces." *Political Science Quarterly,* September 1972.

Ianni, Octavio. "Los Estados Unidos y el militarismo latinoamericano." *Revista Mexicana de Sociologia,* no. 3 (1968).

Inter-American Development Bank. *El progreso económico social en América Latina.* Reports from 1980–1982.

Janowitz, Morris. *The Professional Soldier.* New York: Free Press, 1960.

————. *The Military in the Political Development of New Nations.* Chicago: University of Chicago Press, 1964.

Jaworski, Helan. "Perú: La política internacional del gobierno militar peruano en dos vertientes (1968 a 1980)." Paper presented at the seminar, Políticas exteriores latinoamericanas, Viña del Mar, Chile, September 1982.

Jervis, Robert. "Hypothesis on Misperceptions." *World Politics,* April 1968.

————. *Perceptions and Misperceptions in International Politics.* Princeton, N.J.: Princeton University Press, 1976.

Johnson, John J. "The Latin American Military as a Competing Group in Transitional Society." In John J. Johnson, *The Role of the Military in Underdeveloped Countries.* Princeton, N.J.: Princeton University Press, 1962.

Klare, Michael. *War Without End.* New York: Vintage Books, 1972.

Klare, Michael, and Nancy Stein. *Armas y poder en América Latina.* Mexico City: Edicones ERA, 1978.

Klich, Ignacio F. "L'Amérique Latine, principal client de l'industrie d'armement israelienne." *Le Monde Diplomatique,* September 1980.

Kohler, George. "Toward a General Theory of Armaments." *Journal of Peace Research,* no. 2 (1979).

Lechner, Norbert, ed. *Estado y política en América Latina.* Mexico City: Siglo XXI, 1981.

Levin, Bob, and Larry Rohter. "Brazil: A Call to Arms." *Newsweek*, February 26, 1979.

Lietaer, Bernard. *L'Amérique Latine et l'Europe demain: Le role des multinationales européennes dans les années 1980*. Paris: Presses Universitaires de France, 1980.

Lieuwin, Edwin. "The Changing Role of the Military in Latin America." *Journal of Interamerican Studies*, October 1961.

———. "Militarism and Politics in Latin America." In John J. Johnson, *The Role of the Military in Underdeveloped Countries*. Princeton, N.J.: Princeton University Press, 1962.

———. *The Latin American Military*. Washington, D.C.: Government Printing Office, 1967.

———. "The Changing Role of the Armed Forces: An Analysis." In Robert Tomasek, ed., *Latin American Politics*. New York: Doubleday, 1968.

Lock, Peter. "La dinámica armamentista: Punto nodal en las estratégias de desarrollo." *El Día* (Mexico), October 26, 1981.

Loftus, Joseph E. *Latin American Defense Expenditures, 1938–1965*. Santa Monica, Calif.: RAND Corporation, 1980.

Lowenthal, Abraham F. "Armies and Politics in Latin America: A Review Article." *World Politics*, October 1974.

Lowenthal, Abraham, ed. *Armies and Politics in Latin America*. New York: Holmes and Meier, 1976.

Luckham, Robin. "A Comparative Typology of Civil-Military Relations." *Government and Opposition*, Winter 1971.

———. "Militarism: Arms and the Internationalization of Capital." *IDS Bulletin* (UK) 8, no. 3 (March 1977).

Lumsden, Malvern. "Militarism: Cultural Dimensions of Militarization." Paper presented at the Pugwash Symposium on Militarism, Oslo, November 1977.

Lyautey, Luis Hubert Gonzalve. "Du rôle social de l'officier." *Revue des Deux Mondes*, March 15, 1881.

Lydenberg, Steven. *The U.S. Corporate Role in International Arms Transfers, Weapons for the World Update Report*. New York: Council on Economic Priorities, 1977.

McAlister, Lester. "Civil-Military Relations in Latin America." *Journal of Interamerican Studies*, July 1961.

McKinlay, R. D., and A. S. Cohen. "Performance and Instability in Military and Non-Military Regime Systems." *American Political Science Review*, September 1976.

McRae, Kenneth D. *Consociational Democracy: Political Accommodation in Segmented Societies*. Toronto: McClelland & Stewart, 1974.

Marshall, Jorge. "Gasto público en Chile." *Estudios* (CIEPLAN, Santiago) no. 5 (1981).

Mercado-Jarrín, Edgardo. "La politica de seguridad integral." *Revista del CIMP* (Peru), July-September 1968.

Milenki, Edward S. "Arms Production and National Security in Argentina." *Journal of Interamerican Studies*, August 1980.

Morgenthau, Hans. *La lucha por el poder y la paz*. Buenos Aires: Ed. Sudamericana, 1963.

Morris, Michael, and Victor Millán. *Controlling Latin American Conflicts*. Boulder, Colo.: Westview Press, 1983.

Moyano, Miguel Angel. *Armas modernas para América Latina*. Buenos Aires: Nemont Ediciones, 1981.

National Council of Science and Technology. *Mexico's Programme for Science and Technology, 1978–1982.* Mexico City, n.d.

Needler, Martin. "The Latin American Military: Predatory Reactionaries or Modernizing Patriots." *Journal of Interamerican Studies,* April 1969.

―――. "The Military Withdrawal from Power in South America." *Armed Forces and Society,* Summer 1980.

Nina, A. "La doctrina de seguridad nacional." *Nueva Sociedad,* November-December 1976.

Nordingler, Eric. "Soldier in Mufti." *American Political Science Review,* December 1970.

Nun, José. "El golpe militar de la clase media en América Latina." In Claudio Veliz, *El conformismo en América Latina.* Santiago: Editorial Universitaria, 1970.

Nunn, Frederic. "El profesionalismo militar chileno en el siglo XX." *Cuadernos del Instituto de Ciencias Políticas* (Universidad Católica de Chile), no. 9 (March-April 1976).

O'Donnell, Guillermo. "Modernización y golpes militares: Teoría, comparación y el caso argentino." *Desarrollo Económico,* October-December 1972.

―――. "Modernization and Bureaucratic Authoritarianism: Studies in South American Politics." Berkeley: Institute of International Studies, University of California, 1973.

―――. "Acerca del corporativismo y la cuestión del Estado." Documento CEDES/G.E. CLACSO/no 2. Buenos Aires, 1975.

―――. "Las fuerzas armadas y el estado autoritario del Cono Sur de América Latina." In Norbert Lechner, ed., *Estado y política en América Latina.* Mexico City: Siglo XXI, 1981.

Olmedo, Raul. "Armamentismo y ciclo económico." *Nueva Política* (Mexico), no. 5-6 (April-September 1977).

"Pacto amazónico: Dominación o integración." *Nueva Sociedad* (Caracas), no. 37 (July-August 1979).

Pinochet, Augusto. *Geopolítica.* Santiago: Ed. Andrés Bello, 1974.

Portales, Carlos, and Augusto Varas. "La carrera armamentista en América del Sur." *Mensaje* (Santiago), January-February 1979.

Potash, Robert A. *The Army and Politics in Argentina: 1945–1962, Peron to Frondizi.* Stanford, Calif.: Stanford University Press, 1980.

Powell, Duncan. "Military Assistance and Militarism in Latin America." *Western Political Quarterly,* June 1965.

Price, Robert. "A Theoretical Approach to Military Rule in New States." *World Politics,* April 1971.

Puig, Juan Carlos. "Política internacional Argentina." Paper presented at the seminar, Políticas exteriores comparadas de América Latina, Caracas, October 4-6, 1982.

Pye, Lucian. "Armies in the Process of Political Modernization." In John J. Johnson, *The Role of the Military in Underdeveloped Countries.* Princeton, N.J.: Princeton University Press, 1965.

Rankin, Richard. "The Expanding Institutional Concerns of Latin American Military Establishment: A Review Article." *Latin American Research Review,* Spring 1974.

Rapoport, Anatol. *Fights, Games and Debates.* Ann Arbor: University of Michigan Press, 1960.

―――. "Strategic Thinking in Theoretical Perspective." Typescript, 1980.

Rapoport, David. "A Comparative Theory of Military and Political Types." In Samuel Huntington, *Changing Patterns of Military Politics*. New York: Free Press, 1962.

Rencoret, Gerardo Cortes. "Los tratados de armamentos en América." *Seguridad Nacional* (Santiago), January-March 1978.

Rockefeller, Nelson A. *The Rockefeller Report on the Americas*. Chicago: Quadrangle Books, 1969.

Rodriguez, N. "Seguridad nacional en el Ecuador." *Revista de las Fuerzas Armadas*, May 1978.

Rojas, Jaime, and José Antonio Viera-Gallo. "La doctrina de la seguridad nacional y la militarización de la política en América Latina." *Casa de Chile* (Mexico), 1977.

Rouquié, Alain. "L'Hypotése 'Bonapartiste' et l'émergence des systèmes politiques semi-competitifs." *Révue Française des Sciences Politiques* 25, no. 6 (December 1975).

———. *Les états militaire de Amérique Latine*. Paris: Editions du Seuil, 1982.

Ruhl, Mark. "Colombia: Armed Forces and Society." Latin American Series, Maxwell School of Citizenship and Public Affairs, Syracuse University, New York, 1980.

Russett, Bruce. *Power and Community in World Politics*. San Francisco: W.H. Freeman, 1974.

Ruz, M. "Doctrina de seguridad nacional en América Latina." *Mensaje* (Santiago), August 1977.

Saieh, Alvaro. "Un análisis sobre la posibilidad de evaluar la solvencia crediticia de los países en desarrollo." *Cuadernos de la CEPAL*, no. 36 (1980).

Senghaas, Dieter. "Toward an Analysis of Threat Policy in International Relations." In Klaus von Beyme, ed., *German Political Studies*, vol. 1. London: Sage Publications, 1974.

Shils, Edward. "The Military in the Political Development of New States." In John J. Johnson, *The Role of the Military in Underdeveloped Countries*. Princeton, N.J.: Princeton University Press, 1965.

Smith, Dan, and Ron Smith. "Military Expenditure, Resources and Development." Mimeograph, April 1980.

Smith, Peter. "Argentina: The Uncertain Warriors." *Current History*, February 1980.

Stockholm International Peace Research Institute (SIPRI). *The Arms Trade with the Third World*. Harmondsworth, Eng.: Penguin Books, 1975.

———. *Armaments or Disarmament? The Crucial Choice*. Solna: Tryckindustri, 1979.

———. *World Armaments and Disarmament Yearbook, 1978–1983*. London: Taylor and Francis, 1978–1983.

Stokes, William. "Violence as a Power Factor in Latin American Politics." In Robert Tomasek, comp., *Latin American Politics*. New York: Doubleday, 1966.

Sutton, John L., and Geoffrey Kemp. "Arms to Developing Countries: 1945–1965." *Adelphi Papers*, October 1966.

Thompson, William R. "Systematic Change and the Latin American Military Coup." *Comparative Political Studies*, January 1975.

———. "Regime Vulnerability and the Military Coup." *Comparative Political Studies*, October 1976.

Tomasek, Robert, ed. *Latin American Politics*. New York: Doubleday, 1968.

Torres-Rivas, Edelberto. "La nación: Problemas teóricos e históricos." In Norbert Lechner, ed., *Estado y política en América Latina*. Mexico City: Siglo XXI, 1981.

Tuomi, Helena, and Raimo Väyrynen. *Transnational Corporations, Armaments and Development*. Tampere, Finland: Tampere Peace Research Institute, 1980.

United Nations. *Las consecuencias económicas y sociales de la carrera de armamentos y de los gastos militares*. New York: United Nations, 1972, 1978.

U.S. Arms Control and Disarmament Agency (ACDA). *World Military Expenditures and Arms Transfers 1965–1974*. Washington, D.C.: Government Printing Office, 1976.

————. *World Military Expenditures and Arms Transfers, 1969–1978*. Washington, D.C.: Government Printing Office, 1980.

————. *World Military Expenditures and Arms Transfers, 1971–1980*. Washington, D.C.: Government Printing Office, 1983.

U.S. Congressional Research Service, Library of Congress (various authors). *Implications of President Carter's Conventional Arms Transfer Policy*, 77-223, F, VA 15, U.S., September 22, 1977.

U.S. Department of Defense. *Congressional Presentation, Security Assistance Program FY 1979, 1978*. Washington, D.C.: DoD, 1978.

————. Defense Security Assistance Agency. *Foreign Military Sales and Military Assistance Facts*. Washington, D.C.: DoD, December 1977.

U.S. House of Representatives. Hearings Before the Subcommittee on Inter-American Affairs of the Committee on International Relations, *Arms Trade in the Western Hemisphere*. Washington, D.C.: Government Printing Office, 1978.

U.S. Senate. Select Committee to Study Governmental Operations with Respect to Intelligence Activities. *Alleged U.S. Involvement in Assassination Plots in Five Foreign Countries*. Washington, D.C.: Government Printing Office, 1975.

————. Select Committee to Study Governmental Operations with Respect to Intelligence Activities. *Covert Action in Chile, 1963–1973*. Washington, D.C.: Government Printing Office, 1975.

U.S. Senate. Hearing Before the Committee on Foreign Relations, *Proposed Sale of F-16's to Venezuela*. Washington, D.C.: Government Printing Office, 1982.

Van Klaveren, Alberto. "Instituciones consociativas y estabilización democrática: Alternativas para Chile?" CED (Santiago), Document no. 6, 1983.

Varas, Augusto. "Estudio comparativo de las doctrinas de seguridad nacional en algunos países de América Latina." *Proyecto de Investigación*. FLACSO, Santiago, 1976.

————. "Las nuevas relaciones de poder en América Latina." *APSI* (Santiago), July 28–August 10, 1981.

————. "La reinserción de América Latina en el marco estratégico mundial." *Estudios Internacionales* (Santiago), October–December 1981.

————. "El nuevo armamentismo latinoamericano: Consecuencia de la guerra de las Malvinas." *APSI* (Santiago), no. 110 (July 1982).

————. "Las relaciones de América Latina con la Unión Soviética: Los casos de Argentina, Brasil, Chile y Perú." Paper presented at the seminar, Comparative Latin American Foreign Policies, Viña del Mar, Chile, September 20–23, 1982.

————. "Militarización, armamentismo y gasto militar en Chile, 1973–1981." *Documento de Trabajo*. FLACSO, Santiago, 1982.

————. "Relaciones hemisfericas e industria militar en América Latina." *Socialismo y Participación* (Lima), no. 17 (1982).

————. "La intervención civil de las fuerzas armadas." In Hugo Frühling, Carlos Portales, and Augusto Varas, *Estado y fuerzas armadas en el proceso político chileno*. Santiago: FLACSO, 1983.

————. "Internacionalización y transnacionalización en América Latina." *Estudios Internacionales* (Santiago), January-March 1984.

Varas, Augusto, and Felipe Agüero. *El proyecto político militar*. Santiago: FLACSO, 1984.

Varas, Augusto, and Fernando Bustamante. *Fuerzas armadas y política en Ecuador*. Quito: Editora Latinoamericana, 1978.

Varas, Augusto, Felipe Agüero, and Fernando Bustamante. *Chile, democracia, y fuerzas armadas*. Santiago, Chile: FLACSO, 1980.

Varas, Augusto, Carlos Portales, and Felipe Agüero. "National and International Dynamic of South American Armamentism." *Current Research on Peace and Violence* (Finland) 1 (1980).

Väyrynen, Raimo. "Las corporaciones transnacionales y la transferencia de armas." In CIDE, *La dependencia militar latinoamericana*. Mexico City: CIDE, 1978.

————. "International Patent System, Technological Dominance and Transnational Corporations." In Kirsten Worm, ed., *Industrialization, Development and the Demands for a New International Economic Order*. Copenhagen: Samfundsvidenskabeligt Forlag, 1978.

————. *The Transfer of Arms and Military Technology as an Aspect of Global Militarization*. Paper prepared for the Womp II meeting in Poona, India, July 2–11, 1978.

————. "Restraints of the International Transfer of Arms and Military Technology." *Alternatives* 3 (1978).

————. *The Apartheid System, Militarization and Conflict Formations in South Africa*. IPRA/University of Tokyo-Unesco, 1980. Mimeo.

Veliz, Claudio. *The Centralist Tradition in Latin America*. Princeton, N.J.: Princeton University Press, 1980.

Vicaría de la Solidaridad. "Sobre la actual ideología de la seguridad nacional." Santiago: Arzobispado, 1977.

Villareal, René. "Problemas y perspectivas del comercio y las finanzas internacionales: Los puntos de vista del Sur." *El Trimestre Económico* (Mexico), October-December 1981.

Villegas, Osiris. *Políticas y estrategias para el desarrollo y la seguridad nacional*. Buenos Aires: Pleamar, 1969.

Von Chrismar, Julio C. *Leyes que se deducen del estudio de la expansión de los estados*. Santiago: Memorial del Ejército, 1975.

Von der Goltz, Colmar. *El pueblo en armas*. N.p., 1883.

Von Ludendorff, Erick. *La guerra total*. Buenos Aires: Ediciones Pleamar, 1964.

Wallace, M. D. "Old Nails in New Coffins: The Para Bellum Hypothesis Revisited." *Journal of Peace Research* (Oslo), no. 1 (1981).

Wallensteen, Peter, Johan Galtung, and Carlos Portales, eds. *Global Militarization*. Boulder, Colo.: Westview Press, 1984.

Weaber, James L. "Arms Transfers to Latin America: A Note on the Contagion Effect." *Journal of Peace Research* (Oslo), no. 3 (1974).

Weigest, Hans. *Antología geopolítica*. Buenos Aires: Editorial Pleamar, 1975.

Wesson, Robert. *New Military Politics in Latin America*. New York: Praeger, 1982.

Whaley, B. "Toward a General Theory of Deception." *Journal of Strategic Studies*, March 1982.

Wiarda, Howard. *Corporatism and National Development in Latin America*. Boulder, Colo.: Westview Press, 1981.

Winkelman, Colin, and Brent Merril. "United States and Brazilian Military Relations." *Military Review*, June 1983.

Wyckoff, Theodore. "The Role of the Military in Latin American Politics." In John D. Marts, *The Dynamic of Change in Latin American Politics*. New York: Prentice-Hall, 1965.

Titles in This Series

The Exclusive Economic Zone: A Latin American Perspective, edited by Francisco Orrego Vicuña

†*The Third World Coalition in International Politics,* Second, Updated Edition, Robert A. Mortimer

Militarization and the International Arms Race in Latin America, Augusto Varas

†*Latin American Nations in World Politics,* edited by Heraldo Muñoz and Joseph S. Tulchin

Other Titles of Interest from Westview Press

Political Change in Central America: Internal and External Dimensions, edited by Wolf Grabendorff, Heinrich-W. Krumwiede, and Jörg Todt

†*FOREIGN POLICY on Latin America, 1970–1980,* edited by the staff of Foreign Policy

†*Latin American Foreign Policies: Global and Regional Dimensions,* edited by Elizabeth G. Ferris and Jennie K. Lincoln

†*The New Cuban Presence in the Caribbean,* edited by Barry B. Levine

Colossus Challenged: The Struggle for Caribbean Influence, edited by H. Michael Erisman and John D. Martz

Sovereignty in Dispute: The Falklands/Malvinas, 1493–1982, Fritz L. Hoffmann and Olga Mingo Hoffmann

†*Latin America and the U.S. National Interest: A Basis for U.S. Foreign Policy,* Margaret Daly Hayes

†*The Caribbean Challenge: U.S. Policy in a Volatile Region,* edited by H. Michael Erisman

Modern Weapons and Third World Powers, Rodney W. Jones and Steven A. Hildreth

National Security in the Third World, Abdul-Monem M. Al-Mashat

American Intervention in Grenada: The Implications of Operation "Urgent Fury," edited by Peter M. Dunn and Bruce W. Watson

†Available in hardcover and paperback.

About the Book and Author

Militarization and the International Arms Race in Latin America

Augusto Varas

Military conflicts and dictatorships in Latin America are the main consequences of the increasingly autonomous role of the armed forces in the region, asserts noted scholar Augusto Varas, and international factors related to the expansion of weapon industries in the North and the increasing flow of financial resources to Latin America are accelerating the arms race. Varas discusses the historical function of the armed forces in local politics, the new ideology of the "national security doctrine," and the process of conflict perception by the Latin American military. He also analyzes the inevitable relations between the arms race and the political role of the region's armed institutions. Using Chile as an example, he places these factors in context and illustrates how political crisis can escalate into a regional arms race. He then concludes with a discussion of the links between prospects for democracy in the region and demilitarization and disarmament.

Augusto Varas is a professor at FLACSO (Latin American Faculty of Social Sciences), Santiago, Chile. He has served as a consultant to UNESCO's division of human rights, the UN University, and the Stockholm International Peace Research Institute.

Index